GRAIN FREE HAVEN

THE COOKBOOK:
KETO. PALEO. FOR OUR HEARTS AND KIDS.

MARY ANNE YOUNG

CABIN FEVER PRESS

Copyright © 2018 Mary Anne Young
All Rights Reserved

ISBN: 978-1984268648

Photos by Mary Anne Young
Book design and editing by David Haywood Young

Contents

Dedication ix
Introduction xi

Appetizers & Snacks — 1

Parmesan Crisps 3
Nutty Chocolate 5
Protein Bars 5
Dolmas 7
Jalapeño Poppers 11
Cheese Stuffed Jalapeños 15
Mini Pizza Pucks 17
Smorgastarta...sorta 21

Dressings & Sauces — 25

Mayonnaise 27
Greek Dressing 29
Ranch Dressing 31
Tzatziki 33
Ketchup 35

Breakfasts — 37

Scotch Eggs 39
Bacon Muffins 41
Breakfast Mix 43
Fluffy Pancakes 45

Soups — 47

Posole 49
Mushroom Goat Cheese Soup 53
Vegetable Cheese Soup 57

Broccoli Beer Cheese Soup	59
Two Day Chicken Vegetable Soup	61

Vegetables 65

Mashed Cauliflower	67
Yellow Mashed Cauliflower	71
Broccoli Cauliflower Mash	73
Cauliflower Mac Bake	75
Cauliflower Fritters	77
Soupless Green Bean Casserole	79
Spaghetti Squash Pizza Bake	81
Zucchini Lasagna	85
Sauteed Squash Strings	89
Baked Zucchini Wedges	91
Roasted Acorn Squash	93
Portobello Pizzas	95
Crispy Baked Chips	97
Jicama Fries	99
Coleslaw	101

Chicken 103

Crispy Baked Chicken	105
Mustard Parmesan Wings	107
Pecan Crusted Chicken	109
Chicken Faux Fried Rice	111

Beef 115

Rootless Pot Roast	117
Shepherd's Pie With Mashed Cauliflower	119
Cheesy Burger Bombs	123
Greek Burgers	125
Swedish Meatballs	129
Little Cheesy Meatballs	133
Vegetable Meatloaf	135
Mediterranean Meatloaf	137

Pork — 139

Cornless Tamales	141
Stuffed Poblano Peppers	145
Creamy Coated Pork Chops	149
Stuffed Portobello Mushrooms	151

Seafood — 153

Salmon Stuffed Mushrooms	155
Salmon Patties	157
Creamy Shrimp Alfredo	161
Shrimp with Lemon Cream Sauce	165

Breads & Crusts — 169

Grain Free Pizza Crust	171
Almond Pizza Crust	175
Bred Bread	179
Power (Paleo) Bread	183
Robust Tortillas	185
Quick Muffins	187
Cinnamon Rolls	189
Cranberry Chestnut Muffins	193
Blueberry Muffins	195
Jalapeño Cheddar Muffins	197
Pumpkin Spice Muffins	199
Banana Bread	201
Acorn Squash Bread	203
Cornless Cornbread	205
Cornless Corndogs	207

Desserts — 209

Sugar Free Chocolate Bar	211
Coconut Macaroons	213
Chocolate Cake	215
German Chocolate Cake	217

Apple Strawberry Crisp	219
Strawberry Shortcake	221
Strawberry Lemon Cake With Frosting	225
Chocolate Cheesecake	229
Limey Cheesecake	233
King Cheesecake	237
Pumpkin Pie	243
Double Chocolate Cupcakes	245
Strawberry Cupcakes	247
King Cakelettes	249
Pumpkin Custard	253

Beverages 255

Eggnog	257
Hot Cocoa Mix	259

Afterword 261

DEDICATION

This special book would never have existed without my husband and life partner, David Haywood Young. We worked together to fill a need, and it has changed our lives in so many ways. Thank you, David, for making sure my life is never boring!

Introduction

Welcome to my first cookbook!

Many years ago my husband (the writer David Haywood Young, known as "Big D" in this book) discovered, after a period of debilitating illness, that he is highly sensitive to gluten. Further, even gluten free grains did not do much to help his digestion or gastrointestinal tract. Too much information, maybe, but considering he was (hopefully) less than half way through his life, there were many years ahead of eating. We had to figure out a long term strategy.

Our first step was research, like we do with all of our joint projects. Research revealed more than just grain alternatives. It also led us to realize that sugar can also be a culprit, resulting in a multitude of health problems. There is a lot of information in the world touting the advantages and disadvantages of every food group, condiment and eating style created by man. It was a lot to get through. I am no medical or nutritional professional, but after our research I felt much more prepared to move forward.

Considering the occurrences of cancer, diabetes, and dementia in both our family histories, we decided the best direction for our journey was excluding grains and sugar. This approach does not solve all problems, and to be frank, we have fallen off the wagon here and there over the years. Regardless, it was undeniable that we saw improvements in our health when we stayed on the wagon.

I chose this collection of recipes for a specific reason. When we began avoiding grains and sugar there was a natural drop in cravings, but we still experienced hankerings for foods we loved that typically contained them. We were not surprised by those desires, considering we both spent decades eating them with relish. This recipe collection represents some of our favorite foods, made to fit our grain free and sugar free lifestyle.

Another inspiration to exclude grains and sugar was our daughter (known as Little B in the book). She genetically inherited the potential to develop the same health problems we were trying to manage and avoid, so it was an easy decision to include her in our journey. As she gets older she makes more and more eating decisions for herself. We continue to work to be a good example for her, and hope that a minimum of grains and sugar in her early years will make a lifelong positive impact, even if she eats more of them when older.

Little B also significantly impacted the quality of many recipes—if the food we served her did not leave her with a positive experience it would not have the long term impact on her eating habits we want for her. At this point, she is a lively, healthy eight year old, and only time will tell.

Most of the recipes were previously posted on my food blog, Any Kitchen Will Do (https://anykitchenwilldo.com), which I began in 2012. It is where I shared our journey from grains and sugars to none of either. Over the years we have experimented with different sweeteners and grain alternatives. Some worked well, and some did not. The recipes I chose for this book represent the successes, which I hope will help you on your journey.

All the recipes have been revised and tested so they are consistent with certain tenets:

1) When sweet is added to a recipe it is with fruit or pure stevia powder. We have tried a lot of different sweeteners over the years, some of which have since been shown to cause more problems than sugar. The plant based fiber supplement of pure stevia powder is the healthiest option we know of to add sweet to a dish without raising the glycemic index. It has been used in South America as a sweetener for over a thousand years, and

was finally approved as a dietary supplement in the US in the 1990s. Today it is an accepted and safe ingredient in products available in the US. One more item about stevia: any time I use stevia in a recipe I also include the equivalent for pure cane sugar. For those of you who use sugar, or another type of sweetener, it is the best way I know of to reflect the amount of sweetness added.

2) Not everyone is invested in avoiding grains and sugars. I know that some people will be cooking grain or sugar free for themselves, while serving something else to friends and family. All the recipes I am sharing store well or freeze well. I know from experience that eating in a manner that excludes certain foods means it is sometimes tough to stay on track, so having leftovers easily available is important. Go ahead and cook extra, putting away leftover servings for times when you need them quickly.

3) When you are craving grains or sugar you should figure out what you are actually craving. You may have just cut out grains or sugars from your diet, or did so years ago. Either way, you used to eat differently. There was a simple concept I realized a few years ago when trying to eat healthier. If I was craving a food that is outside my eating realm it was important to figure out exactly what I craved. Was it primarily about the taste, texture, occasion, or appearance? The cravings varied and eventually became less frequent, but made for a fun way of experimenting with foods. You can sate the hankering for the crunch of chips with my Parmesan Crisps. Your craving for pizza can be satisfied with, well, pizza! An oatmeal craving can be taken care of with my Breakfast Mix. A desire for macaroni and cheese can be squashed with the Cauliflower Mac Bake and the Zucchini Lasagna can cover almost any pasta desire you may have. Bread? Well there are a number of recipes to take care of that too!

4) Weird ingredients. I already mentioned stevia, which may be new to you. There are also multiple ingredients made from seeds and nuts, which are nutrient dense alternatives to grains. Most of these ingredients are easily available at your local grocery store, either in traditional food aisles or the Nat-

ural or Health aisle. Be aware that if you are gluten sensitive you need to do extra reading on packages. Some products with all gluten free ingredients may be labeled gluten free, but processed in facilities that will result in cross contamination with wheat or other gluten sources. If you are concerned about contamination there are plenty of sources online that offer safe, certified ingredients.

5) Read the whole recipe before starting. Although some recipes are quick and immediately ready, some have multiple steps or need to sit overnight before serving for optimum flavor and texture.

I will stop here and leave the rest to you. My family spent a lot of time in the kitchen to create these recipes, as well as tons of memories, and in the process extend our lives (we hope!) through the healing power of food. I hope this book helps you on your journey!

Appetizers & Snacks

Parmesan Crisps

Dinner one night was some leftover steak. Wonderful stuff, but it looked kind of lonely sitting by itself on the plate. I came up with these crisps, which were quick, fun, and brightened up a dinner made up otherwise of leftovers. Little B and I even took some off the baking sheet early and laid them over some wooden spoon handles. When they cooled they looked like little bitty taco shells. I can't describe how spiffy they tasted when a slice of steak was nestled in one. Our leftover dinner became a little steak and cheese party.

> Grated Parmesan cheese
> Sea salt
> Garlic powder or cayenne pepper powder (if you like a kick)
> Parchment Paper

Preheat oven to 325 degrees. Line shallow baking sheets with parchment paper.

Measure a heaping tablespoon of cheese and drop it onto the paper. Use your finger to spread out the cheese into a round shape of even thickness. Leave about an inch between rounds for possible spreading.

Sprinkle lightly with salt and garlic powder or cayenne pepper powder.

Bake for about five minutes, until the edges begin to brown. Remove pan from oven.

Crisps can be removed from paper after about a minute with a spatula.

If you want to shape them for fancy serving, do so immediately after one minute or they will stay flat. Hang them over the thick handle of a wooden spoon (suspended between two plates) to give a taco shell shape, or press them into a muffin cup to make them little bowls.

1 ounce bitter-sweet chocolate
2 tablespoons butter (or coconut butter for dairy free)
2 tablespoons heavy cream (or coconut/almond milk for dairy free)
3/8 teaspoon pure stevia powder (equivalent to 1/4 cup pure cane sugar)
1/2 cup blanched almond flour
1 teaspoon ground cinnamon
1 1/2 cup mixed raw nuts, finely chopped
 cup unsweetened shredded coconut

Nutty Chocolate Protein Bars

WE HAVE STANDARD staples we take on hikes and overnight trips—nuts, peanut butter, jerky, cheese, boiled eggs. They are convenient, energy-building and filling, but with all our hiking I wanted to add some variety. The chewiness and nuttiness of these bars reminds me of a candy bar you find at the store—rhymes with tickers.

Little B tentatively took a small first bite, then proceeded to eat an entire bar and asked for some in her lunch the next day. Score! This is significant, because in her worldly young brain anything Mommy suggests is immediately suspect. These bars are a tiny bit sticky at room temperature, but what protein bars aren't? They hold together well when wrapped in foil or plastic wrap, so score again! It was easy to add them to the hiking food mix, and quite a treat when taking a break looking out over water and mountains and whales.

Line an 8x8 inch baking dish with foil.

In a medium microwaveable bowl, melt the chocolate and butter on 50 percent power for about 1 minute or until melting and softened. The butter does not have to be fully melted. Remove from microwave and stir until smooth and blended.

Add in the cream, stevia and almond flour. The mixture will be stiff and sticky when well blended. Stir in the nuts and coconut—you may need to use your hands to get it all mixed in, but then your hands will be primed for the next step.

Firmly press the mixture into the bottom of the foil lined pan using the back of a spoon that is lightly coated with oil or butter, or just use your hands.

Chill at least two hours or until firm. Cut into eight large bars or 16 snack squares. Store in refrigerator or freeze.

Dolmas

DOLMA GENERALLY MEANS 'stuffed thing', and depending on where you are in the world, the stuffed thing includes some sort of vegetable—potatoes, squash, peppers, or tomatoes. After room is made in said vegetable they are filled with stuffing made of grains, vegetables and seafood or meat, which is then cooked. In this case we are leaning towards a Greek variation that involves stuffing grape leaves. The grape leaf version of dolmas can be eaten with fork and knife, or picked up as finger food.

To make them grain free we used cauliflower instead of rice. I always like having dolmas as part of a Greek meal—they are great hot or cold, can be made in advance; ideally at least one day before serving so the flavors can marry nicely. I hardly noticed the absence of rice in this version, since the cauliflower gave them a very similar texture to grain or rice.

- 1 8-ounce jar grape leaves
- 1/2 head raw cauliflower
- 1/2 cup pine nuts (optional)
- 1/2 cup raisins (optional)
- 1 pound raw ground lamb
- 1/2 medium raw onion
- 2 tablespoons fresh mint
- 1/2 cup fresh parsley leaves
- 2 garlic cloves, crushed
- 1 1/2 teaspoons sea salt
- 1/2 teaspoon ground black pepper
- 2 fresh lemons
- 1 large egg

Carefully remove the leaves from the jar and place in the sink or a large bowl. They are usually tightly rolled together in the jar and can easily be torn. The filling quantity will not be enough for all the leaves, so it is not the end of the world if some get torn or are too small. Gently loosen the roll and cover the leaves with hot water, allowing them to soak at least 15 minutes before rolling into dolmas.

Meanwhile, break the cauliflower into florets, removing the stems. Place the florets in the food processor bowl and pulse until the cauliflower looks like rice. This takes about 10 to 15 one-second pulses. Place riced cauliflower in a large mixing bowl.

(Optional) Heat a dry skillet over medium high heat, then add pine nuts and raisins, stirring often and cooking until the pine nuts are lightly toasted, about 3-5 minutes. Set aside to cool, then coarsely chop. Add the nuts and raisins to the cauliflower in the mixing bowl. Personally, I don't use raisins because in my opinion it makes the dolmas too sweet, but it is a traditional ingredient in the Greek version.

Place the lamb, onion, mint, parsley, garlic, salt, and pepper in the bowl of a food processor and steadily pulse the mixture until the ingredients form a paté texture and everything is combined. I have also used a pastry cutter when a processor is not available—it takes a little longer, but works. Add the lamb paté to the cauliflower and mix well. The easiest way to do this is with your hands.

In a steamer basket or pasta basket that will fit over a larger pot of boiling water, place a few grape leaves—the ones that are torn or small—to mostly cover the bottom of the basket. There can be some gaps.

Put enough water in the pot base so it does not rise above the bottom of the basket. Cut half of one lemon in half and drop the two quarters in the water. Cover and bring the water to a boil while you prepare the dolmas.

Drain the water from the rest of the grape leaves. Place a leaf on a flat surface with the shiny side facing down, veins facing up. Snip off the stem, and place about one mounded tablespoon of filling on the end of the leaf closest to you, where the stem was attached. The filling amount can vary, depending on the size of the leaf you are using. Roll from the bottom until the filling is covered by one layer of leaf. Fold in the side leaf flaps and keep rolling until you have a cigar shape.

You want to roll them pretty tightly so they don't come apart during the cooking process. This is different from traditional dolmas where you want to leave a little wiggle room for the rice to expand during cooking. The cauliflower actually shrinks as it cooks, so roll them up tight, but be gentle and don't tear the leaves!

Place the rolls in the pan on the long end (lying down) and nestle them up against each other as more are made. There can be multiple layers if needed, but place the higher layers crosswise to the lower layer so air can circulate between them. They will all get cooked.

Cut half of one lemon into thin slices circles and arrange the slices on top of the highest layer of dolmas in the steamer. Place the filled basket over the boiling water. Cover with a lid, turn the heat down to low and get a gentle simmer going. Cook 25-30 minutes, until the leaves are tender but not falling apart.

Remove from heat. Separate the steamer portion and pour out the water from the base pot. Replace the steamer in the base.

In a small bowl, whisk the juice from the remaining lemon with the egg until frothy. Remove lemon slices from the top of the dolmas. Pour the frothy mixture over the dolmas, then put the lid back on and let the sauce set. You do not have to put them back on heat. The hot dolmas gently cook the egg/lemon sauce to create a tangy coating.

The sauce will set in about ten minutes. When done remove the dolmas from the pan, place covered in the fridge, and wait until they're chilled before serving. They taste great whether cold, room temperature, or hot. They are best if reheated the day after preparation, rather than eaten immediately when they come out of the pan.

8-10 large jalapenos (as straight as you can find)
8 ounces cream cheese
1/2 cup grated cheddar cheese
2 egg whites
1 cup golden flaxseed meal
1 teaspoon garlic powder
1 teaspoon ground cumin
1 teaspoon salt
Ranch Dressing for serving

Jalapeño Poppers

During the first year of my blog I made some addictive jalapeño popper dip. It had the stuffed jalapeño taste and we spread it bumpily on almost everything until the last spoonful was gone. After finding jalapeños on sale at the store the other day I decided it was time to again delve into the jalapeño popper world, with the intent of creating a more original result.

We have experimented with finding a coating that bakes up crisp during our foray into making Scotch Eggs. Confident in our knowledge from many egg batches, we applied the same idea to these poppers. Instead of making it easy on ourselves by cutting the peppers in half and stuffing them, we wanted them whole, but also breaded! Why not keep it simple and wrap them in bacon? Hmmm...bacon. Not this time! Much too easy and predictable. We wanted to taste the peppers, which would be harder if the bacon was involved. It is a very domineering ingredient, although it goes with almost anything. Now I want some bacon...but on to the bacon-less poppers!

The filling stayed in the poppers and helped them keep their shape. The breading stayed stuck, and boy did we taste the peppers! We expected a varying level of heat among the peppers, as is typical, but Big D got quite a surprise. He must have bit into a seed cluster juuuuust right, for he went running for a drink, then dove for a piece of bread, where he finally found relief. It is rare when he gets overheated by spice, much less have tears well in his eyes because of them. I had no such biting surprise, but really enjoyed noshing on the poppers and relished their return to our growing list of things-we-gave-up-and-missed-but-now-have-back-again. Yay!

Preheat oven to 350 degrees.

Lay jalapeños on a flat surface and figure out which side they rest on most stably. On the side opposite of the resting side cut a narrow opening that stops short of both ends lengthwise—narrow enough to keep the stuffing in, but wide enough to clean out the seeds and pulp from inside the pepper. Leave the stem attached. With a small spoon or narrow knife gently scrape out some seeds and pulp, making room for the stuffing. Set aside the jalapeños.

In a medium bowl place the cream cheese and cheddar cheese. Heat in microwave on 50% power for one minute, and repeat until softened. Add 1/2 teaspoon garlic powder, 1/2 teaspoon cumin and 1/2 teaspoon sea salt and stir until ingredients are combined.

Using a small spoon gently push cheese mixture into the jalapeños until they are full, or the filling is used up.

Place the egg whites in a medium bowl and whisk until slightly foamy but not stiff. In another bowl combine the flaxseed meal, 1/2 teaspoon garlic powder, 1/2 teaspoon cumin and 1/2 teaspoon salt.

Dip each stuffed jalapeño in egg whites, then roll in flaxseed mixture until well coated, pressing some of the meal against the pepper where it does not instantly cling. Gently place coated jalapeños in a small baking dish (8x8 or 9x9), with a little space between.

Bake for about 50 minutes, until coating browns and peppers are soft. Remove and let cool for at least five minutes. Serve with ranch dressing or other dipping sauce.

6 large jalapeños
8 ounces cream cheese, room temperature
4 ounces ham, finely diced
1 teaspoon garlic powder
1/2 cup finely shredded Mexican cheese blend
    (or Monterrey jack and sharp cheddar)

Cheese Stuffed Jalapeños

I considered doing something fancy and complicated for my food blog's first anniversary, but that was not where I was in life at the time. What I came up with was a simple, quiet pepper gem with some bite.

This recipe is consistent with our grain free eating, and was made to celebrate me and Big D, who has been so supportive of my creative outlet of a blog, especially with tweakful suggestions and acting as guinea pig.

Poor Little B was pretty much left out of this one, since she is not interested in jalapeños. Spicy and cheesy and addictive these are.

Preheat oven to 400 degrees.

Prepare jalapeños by removing stems, slicing in half lengthwise and scraping out seeds and membrane.

Combine cream cheese, garlic and ham together. Fill the jalapeño halves with the mixture.

Sprinkle each jalapeño half with the Mexican cheese blend, gently pressing it into the filled halves. On a shallow baking sheet arrange the jalapeños so there is some space between them.

Bake for 20-25 minutes until cheese is melted and browning, possibly drizzling down the sides of the jalapeños.

Serve immediately or let cool and serve at room temperature.

Mini Pizza Pucks

Our whole family loves pizza. These pizza pucks I made are a result of spontaneous experimentation. They were quick, fun, and Little B enjoyed helping making them, of course.

I call them pizza pucks, not because they are overly hard or difficult to eat, but because you can pack them up, like pucks.

Besides being a good dinner, the leftovers worked well as a cold snack on the way to Little B's soccer practice, or whatever happens after five but before bedtime that does not involve crashing on the couch at home. What better snack than some protein before running around for an hour or more?

- 3 cups shredded mozzarella and cheddar cheese
- 1/2 cup golden flaxseed meal
- 1 egg
- 1 tablespoon dried parsley leaves
- 1 tablespoon dried basil leaves
- 1 teaspoon garlic powder
- 1 teaspoon sea salt
- 1 cup large black olives
- 6 roasted or pickled garlic cloves (you can use raw or garlic powder instead)
- 20-30 slices pepperoni
- 1/2 cup Parmesan cheese

Preheat oven to 350 degrees. In a food processor combine olives and garlic, then pulse until a rough paste forms. Set aside.

In a medium bowl combine the mozzarella and cheddar cheeses with flaxseed meal. Whisk the egg and add to cheese mixture, folding it in until the cheese is coated. Add the salt, parsley, basil and garlic powder, doing a final few stirs to distribute the spices.

On two nonstick cookie sheets make flat piles of cheese, about 2 inches in diameter with about an inch between them. Spoon about 1 tablespoon of olive paste on each pile, spreading it gently with the bottom of the spoon.

Place one to two slices of pepperoni on each pile, then sprinkle with Parmesan cheese.

Bake in the oven (using two different rack levels) for 12-15 minutes, until the edges of cheese begin to brown and the pepperoni glistens. Remove from oven and let cool for five minutes before serving.

24 equally thick slices Power Bread (about 1/4 inch; need
    1 1/2 loaves)
1/2 cup Butter or Ghee (room temperature)
4 ounces thin sliced ham (about 15 slices)
4 ounces thin sliced turkey (about 15 slices)
8 ounces thin sliced cheese
1 English cucumber, peeled and sliced thin
7 cups diced chicken (about seven chicken breasts)
1 cup mayonnaise
1 cup diced dill pickle
1/4 cup shredded onion
1 teaspoon curry
24 ounces cream cheese (room temperature)
16 ounces sour cream (room temperature)
1 large round tomato
10-14 leaves of green/purple lettuce or flat leaf parsley
    sprigs
3 boiled eggs (10 minute boil), chilled
1 tall red or yellow bell pepper
1 bunch green onions
1 large carrot
 2-3 mint or basil leaves
 Salt and pepper to taste

Smorgastarta...Sorta

Making a dramatic centerpiece of a meal is fun, and this recipe definitely fills the bill. It can also be made in advance so there is not a lot of last minute rushing around. This is my version of a smorgastarta. If you have never heard of such a thing, it is basically a layered sandwich frosted like a cake.

The original version is popular in Sweden and served at parties—bread, herring mousse, cucumber, bread, smoked salmon, sauce, lettuce, bread, then frosted with a cream cheese/sour cream 'frosting.' I make a less traditional version because my traditional audience is not as excited about all the seafood as most Swedes. How can I go wrong with chicken, ham and turkey?

It was really fun to make, much prettier than an old fashioned sandwich tray, and deeeelicious! The leftover bits and pieces from the garnish made a great salad.

The recipe can be halved for a smaller crowd. The full recipe easily filled up a dozen people.

Make sandwich decorations and chill them while constructing cake:

To make chicken salad combine chicken, mayonnaise, pickle, shredded onion and curry. Set aside.

Remove crust from all slices of bread, making the corners squared off as much as possible so they will fit together uniformly. Butter one side of eight pieces of bread and place them butter side up in a rectangular shape on a serving tray. The butter will prevent the layer of bread from getting soggy. Spread chicken salad on bread, bringing as close to the edges as possible. Place a layer of cucumber on top of the chicken salad.

Butter both sides of eight pieces of bread and place on top of the cucumber. Arrange ham and turkey in loose rolls on bread, making sure meat slices are not pressed flat, and lining them up with the outer edges of the 'cake.' Drizzle mustard over meat. Add a layer of cheese. Butter one side of eight pieces of bread and place butter side down on top of cheese.

Thoroughly blend together the cream cheese and sour cream until smooth. Use the mixture like frosting and cover the sandwich on top and all sides.

Press parsley sprigs or lettuce fans on side of frosted sandwich so they stick up slightly taller than the top of the 'cake.' Arrange egg slices, radishes, carrots, green onions, tomato roses and bell pepper rings on top to decorate. Chill sandwich for at least three hours before serving.

Dressings & Sauces

1 egg yolk
1 egg
1 cup avocado oil
2 tablespoons lemon juice
1/4 – 1/2 teaspoon sea salt

Mayonnaise

Since I was a kid I've always liked the taste of mayonnaise: the smooth creaminess it gave to sandwiches, sauces and recipes. I fondly remember lunching on many ham and cheese sandwiches layered with tomatoes, pickles and a nice combination of mayo and mustard mixed up with it all. The sandwiches, along with the occasional dollop on a tomato or tossing it in tuna salad, bring back memories of hot summer days, and loud lunches in school cafeterias.

I am particular about my mayonnaise. I like it tart and creamy. Our first forays into making mayonnaise tasted good but were not quite a replacement for the flavor of my youth. You might not be as picky about the taste as I am, but Big D tried this version recently and it hit the mark! We are pretty sure it is the avocado oil that took it over the edge as a true substitute for my beloved mayo of childhood.

Olive oil works well, too, but the flavor of olive oil takes it in a different direction. This is such an easy recipe that works every time and keeps me away from the store stuff, which is soy-filled, sugar-filled, and preserved with the nasty calcium disodium EDTA.

This mayonnaise can be used in lieu of the store bought mayonnaise, as well as cream or milk in savory sauces. We use it as a base for our beloved Ranch Dressing too!

Place egg yolk and egg in a blender, turning it on medium speed.

Slowly add oil to the eggs in a narrow, steady stream until fully incorporated.

Add lemon juice while the mixture continues to blend.

Stir in salt to desired taste.

Remove mayonnaise to a glass container that can be sealed air-tight. Store in refrigerator.

GREEK DRESSING

Big D brought home some beautiful lamb chops one evening and it started us talking about how good they would be marinated in some olive oil, lemon juice and mint. As we ate the lovely marinated chops we were reminded about how much we enjoyed some of our early experiences with Greek food from a restaurant called John the Greek's in San Antonio, Texas. We especially remembered the Greek Dressing they served and sold (and still do!).

This dressing is tangy with oregano, thyme and lemon dancing around together in my mouth! Not exactly like the stuff by John, but so much better, in my opinion, than other vinaigrettes available at the store, which tend to be too sweet. This dressing really stands up to a salad full of strong flavors like roasted peppers, feta and olives. It also works well as a meat marinade.

>   1/2 cup extra virgin olive oil
>   1/4 cup white or red wine vinegar
>   1/4 cup fresh squeezed lemon juice
>   2 cloves garlic, crushed
>   1 teaspoon dried oregano leaves
>   1/2 teaspoon dried thyme leaves
>   1/2 teaspoon fresh dill
>   1/2-3/4 teaspoon sea salt
>   2 pinches freshly ground black pepper

Add all ingredients except oil into a stainless steel bowl with at least a two cup capacity. Stir with a fork or whisk until well combined.

Continue stirring while adding oil in a thin stream. Stir a bit more after all the oil is added.

Store in a glass jar and let sit overnight in the fridge before using.

About ten minutes before serving pull it out to warm up a bit towards room temperature, since the oil may have formed solids.

Shake well and serve.

Ranch Dressing

Since we began making our own stellar homemade mayonnaise we are confidently surging forward in using it for sauce bases, which includes this lovely dressing. I have always preferred homemade ranch dressing over the bottled stuff, and used to rely on dressing mixes.

When I started reading labels more closely I discovered some mixes have untoward ingredients, like monosodium glutamate. That stuff puffs me up like a balloon. Others have 'modified food starch.' If you look up such an ingredient you may find it can sometimes include wheat, corn or soy. Not fun, especially for Big D with his extreme sensitivity to wheat.

This dressing is quick and easy, making it a staple in our fridge. You can even make the mayonnaise in the blender, then add the dressing ingredients and get it done all at once!

- 1 cup mayonnaise
- 1/2 cup heavy cream (or your preferred non-dairy milk of choice)
- 2 tablespoons lemon juice
- 1 1/2 teaspoon apple cider vinegar
- 1 tablespoon dried onion flakes
- 2 tablespoons fresh parsley, finely chopped
- 1 teaspoon dried basil leaves, crushed
- 1/2 teaspoon black pepper, ground
- 1/2 teaspoon garlic powder
- 2-4 tablespoons water (optional)
- 1/4-1/2 teaspoon sea salt, to taste

In a medium bowl combine all ingredients except salt, then whisk together until well combined. Add salt to taste.

Chill overnight to allow flavors to blend. Store in the refrigerator.

If dressing is too thick after chilling, a bit of water can be added to thin it out.

2 cups plain Greek yogurt (or 1 cup sour cream and 1 cup plain yogurt)
1 medium cucumber
2 large garlic cloves, crushed
1 tablespoon finely chopped fresh mint
2 tablespoons finely chopped fresh dill
1 tablespoon olive oil
2 tablespoons fresh lemon juice
Sea salt, to taste

Tzatziki

I could just eat this stuff straight from a bowl, with a big spoon, as in "Would you like some lamb with your tzatziki?" Forget daintily dipping or drizzling it on food.

Sometimes I get a Greek salad just to be able to mix tzatziki in with it. I used to love dipping pita bread into tzatziki and hummus. What a bite exploding with flavor!

These days, since I don't eat pita anymore, I rely on roasted meats and veggies as my tzatziki conduits. Beyond the lovely, tangy creaminess of the sauce, I just like saying the word—tzatziki, tzatziki, tzatziki.

I eat salsa with Mexican food, I eat wasabi with sushi, I slather steaks with chimichurri, I put mustard on hot dogs and I top Greek food with tzatziki. So there.

Peel the cucumber, then slice in half lengthwise. Remove the seeds from the cucumber, then finely dice. Sprinkle salt on the diced cucumber and toss, then let sit for about five minutes.

Place diced cucumber in between two towels and press gently to remove any excess water. You may need to repeat with more dry towels to get all the water.

In a medium bowl combine yogurt/sour cream, garlic, mint, dill, olive oil and lemon juice. Stir until combined. Fold in cucuber and mix until it is evenly distributed. Add salt to taste.

Chill overnight before serving.

Ketchup

Is it Catsup or Ketchup? I don't know the difference, but I do know that both of them are red, slightly tangy dipping sauces that are mostly tomato.

Once we hosted a slumber party for a young friend and fed them burgers, hot dogs and fries. Our household rarely uses ketchup, so we don't usually have any around. Ack! No red stuff in the fridge! We got some wide-eyed looks from our young guests when we declared the absence of the condiment.

Instead of running to the store I dove into our pantry and attempted to make a batch of it myself. With tomato paste as a base it was easy to combine some spices and vinegar to come up with a pretty darned good version. It seemed to do the trick and the party continued without a hitch. There was indeed tween drama, but not about the ketchup!

- 6 ounces tomato paste
- 1/4 cup white vinegar
- 1 tablespoon garlic powder
- 1 tablespoon onion powder
- Dash allspice
- 1 teaspoon salt
- Dash pure stevia powder (equivalent to 1 tablespoon pure cane sugar)
- 1/2 cup water

Whisk together all ingredients very thoroughly. Serve immediately or store in the refrigerator until needed.

Breakfasts

1 pound breakfast sausage (we use Jimmy Dean Natural)
8 medium boiled eggs, peeled
1 cup golden flaxseed meal
2 raw eggs
1 teaspoon sea salt

Scotch Eggs

Starting in high school my friends and I would go to the Texas Renaissance Festival every autumn. It ran October through November on weekends. The trip was a big deal for us because it did not include parents. Since we could not get permission (or collect sufficient funds) for an overnight trip, our adventure was a freakishly long marathon. A one way trip from San Antonio to the festival north of Houston was at least four hours. The round trip, plus time at the festival (and staying up late the night before leaving) equaled a twenty-hour day. It was a lot of fun and a lot of gas station stops. We returned home tired and smelly and happy, with bags smelling of incense and full of Christmas presents.

Our first stop in the festival grounds was always along the right edge of the outer ring, to eat our first of many treats: Scotch eggs. Here is a low carb grain free version that reminds me of the satisfying festival snack.

Preheat the oven to 350 degrees. Line a baking sheet with aluminum foil.
Combine the flaxseed meal and salt together in a bowl.
In another bowl whisk together the two raw eggs.
Divide the sausage into eight piles. Using your hands, press the sausage into a patty in the palm of your hand. Place a hard boiled egg in the middle of the patty and and mold the sausage around it until it is completely and evenly covered.
Roll each sausage-covered egg in the raw egg mix, then roll each in the flaxseed meal to coat it. Repeat with the remaining eggs, then roll them all once more in the meal until it is gone.
Place the eggs on the foil-lined baking sheet, at least two inches apart. Bake the eggs until the outside is browned and the sausage is cooked through, about 25 to 30 minutes.
Remove from the oven and let the eggs rest for 5 minutes.
Slice in half and serve with mustard.
Store leftovers in the refrigerator.

BACON MUFFINS

A nice thing about these eggs is prep time for enjoying such traditional breakfast ingredients drops exponentially. A typical bacon and eggs breakfast requires standing over crackling bacon and gently fondling eggs for 20 minutes or so, while sometimes taking special orders for soft bacon or over easy eggs.

With this dish I did five minutes of prep, got dressed for the day, then sat down and read some Harry Potter to Little B until the oven timer went off. Always looking for more cuddle time! And she insisted they be called Bacon Muffins when I started suggesting other names. Sometimes it is wise not to argue.

> 2 tablespoons butter, cut into 12 pieces
> 12 slices bacon
> 12 eggs
> 1 cup shredded cheese (exclude butter and cheese for dairy free)
> Sea salt and coarse ground black pepper to taste
> Garlic powder, parsley or chili powder for sprinkling (optional)

Preheat oven to 350 degrees.

In a muffin tin that holds twelve muffins (or 12 silicon muffin cups) line each cup with a piece of bacon. For crispier bacon stand the meaty side up with the fat edge down. For less crispy bacon stand the bacon fat side up with meat side down.

Drop a piece of butter in the bottom of each cup. Crack an egg into each cup. Sprinkle on top of the egg salt and pepper and/or or other seasonings like garlic powder, parsley flakes or chili powder.

Sprinkle cheese equally among the twelve cups.

Bake 18 minutes for soft, and up to 21 minutes for firm eggs. Remove from oven and let sit for a few minutes to cool, then serve.

1 cup golden flaxseed meal
1 cup shredded unsweetened coconut
2 cups natural (unblanched) almond meal
2/3 cup chia seeds
1/4 cup ground cinnamon
2 teaspoons sea salt

Breakfast Mix

Before removing grains from our diet my family always relied on oatmeal, as staple on our camping and kayaking trips or a quick breakfast at home. Although our love for the stuff carries on, our desire to avoid grains is now ever present.

The chia seeds are great thickeners, and gave us all serious boosts of energy that lasted pretty much all day, which is very much needed during cold winter days or long hikes. Sometimes we mix in cocoa powder or drop a spoonful of peanut butter for even more protein.

Combine flaxseed meal, coconut, almond meal, chia seeds, cinnamon and salt. Stir until ingredients are well mixed together. Store in an airtight container.

For Single Serving

> 1/2 cup breakfast mix
> 1/2 cup hot water

Optional Add Ins

> 1/4 cup heavy cream or other milk substitute
> Dash of preferred sweetener (optional)
> Nuts or berries (optional)

For a single serving place 1/2 cup of the mixture in a bowl. Add sweetener (if a powder) and stir. Add hot water, sweetener (if liquid) and cream. Stir and let sit for at least one minute to thicken. Add more water to adjust thickness as desired. Eat immediately.

The mix can also be combined with liquid and left in the refrigerator for a grain free version of 'overnight oats.'

1 cup coconut flour
1/2 teaspoon baking soda
1 teaspoon ground cinnamon
1/4 teaspoon pure stevia powder (equivalent to 1/4 cup pure cane sugar)
1/2 teaspoon sea salt
11 medium eggs
1/2 cup coconut oil
1 cup heavy whipping cream (substitute with coconut milk for dairy free version)
Additional fat (oil, lard or butter) for cooking

Fluffy Pancakes

I caution you about eating more than two of these pancakes at a time without at least ten minutes in between servings. They are deceptively filling and seem to expand like sponges in the stomach. Other than being filling, they are a great way to get a healthy breakfast into your family.

    In a medium bowl combine the flour, baking soda, cinnamon, stevia, and salt.
    In a separate mixer bowl* with a whisk attachment place the eggs, coconut oil, and cream. Mix the wet ingredients on medium until combined.
    Add the dry ingredient mixture to the wet and mix on high until well combined and any solid pieces of coconut oil are broken up and incorporated.
    Heat an electric skillet, or a large skillet on the stove to medium high. Add a drop of fat (about a teaspoon of butter, coconut oil or lard) to the pan and let it heat up. Add 1/4-1/3 cup of the batter and gently spread it out into a pancake with approximate diameter of 3"-4".
    Cook for about two minutes until the bottom of the pancake sets, then flip it over with a large spatula. Cook for about two more minutes until both sides are consistently browned.
    Please note that this batter will not have bubbles popping up while the first side is cooking, like traditional pancakes, so don't look for them as a clue for when to flip them.
    Repeat with remaining batter until it is gone.
    Serve immediately or store in the refrigerator or freezer in airtight container.

The batter can also be made in a large blender, but smaller blenders (less than 8 cups) may be too small to hold all the ingredients.

Soups

Toppings

    1 small red onion, chopped
    2 avocados, chopped
    2 limes, cut into 1/8 wedges
    1 bunch radishes, halved and thinly sliced
    1/2 head cabbage, shredded
    1 cup sour cream
    1 cup cheddar cheese, grated
    1 cup cotija cheese, crumbled
    1/2 cup pico de gallo or salsa

Posole

My lovely friend Tammy first introduced me to posole a few years ago. One weekend when we were visiting her, she and her daughter made a batch. It smelled delicious and we had a blast deciding on what toppings were perfect for each one of us. I love her and you will love this soup!

- 2 cups roughly chopped white onion
- 1 cup roughly chopped carrot
- 1 tablespoon paprika
- 1 teaspoon ground cumin
- 1/2 teaspoon ground coriander
- 2 teaspoons dried oregano leaves
- 4 garlic cloves, minced
- 8 cups pork broth (if there is not enough from cooking the pork, add water)
- 1 cup dark beer (I suggest Negro Modelo or a porter), or additional broth
- (Optional) 4-6 cups hominy*, canned (or prepared fresh by simmered in water for two hours, drained)
- 1 pound tomatillos, shucked, rinsed and roughly chopped
- 4 large green chiles, roughly chopped
- 2 limes, juiced with meat included
- Salt to taste

In 8-10 quart stock pot place pork shoulder over high heat. Turn shoulder as each side browns, until all sides have color. Add water and scrape bottom of pan to release browned bits. Cook pork over medium heat until pork easily shreds, about two hours.

Remove pork and liquid from pot and set aside, retaining the liquid separately. When meat is cool enough to handle shred it into bite-sized pieces.

Set heat under the now empty stock pot to medium high and add you high heat fat of choice. When it is melted and hot add the onions and garlic. When they start to sweat add the carrots.

Add paprika, coriander, oregano and cumin. Stir and cook longer until you can smell the spices. Add broth and beer. Cook until the mixture begins to boil softly, about five minutes.

Add to the soup pork, hominy (optional), tomatillos and chiles. Stir and cook until a soft boil begins again. Taste the soup then sprinkle liberally with salt as needed. Stir and taste again—there should be a noticeable flavor difference. if not, add more salt.

Turn heat down to a simmer and cover, making sure there is still a very soft boil. Cook for an additional two hours.

For serving, place toppings in separate bowls with spoons. Serve posole in large soup bowls and pass around the toppings!

Hominy is a type of corn. I included it in this recipe because it is a traditional ingredient. Exclude it if sensitive to grains, or specifically corn.

1 pound white button mushrooms
2 tablespoons butter
1 medium carrot, finely chopped
1 small bunch green onions, finely chopped
1/2 small yellow onion, finely chopped
3 garlic cloves, crushed
1/2 bunch fresh parsley, stems removed
2 teaspoons sea salt
1 teaspoon ground black pepper
3 cups chicken broth
4 ounces goat cheese
1 cup sour cream
Additional salt to taste

Mushroom Goat Cheese Soup

I love mushrooms in all their shapes, sizes and flavors. Joining them with cheese makes my mouth sing. This soup is easy to make and is very satisfying on a cool autumn evening.

I usually like my soup to have some texture, which is why I puréed instead of strained the base. If you like smooth soup I have included a step to make it so.

I also wanted to let the flavors of the non-mushroom vegetables and the goat cheese shine, so I used the more subtle white button mushrooms, which are much less earthy than shiitake or portobellos. If you want a stronger mushroom flavor just use your mushroom of choice instead of the white button I used. Enjoy!

Immediately before making the soup rinse dirt off mushrooms with cold water and leave them out to dry. Remove stems from all the mushrooms. Slice mushroom caps and set aside. Roughly chop up stems.

Melt butter in medium sauce pot over medium high heat.

When butter is bubbling add green onions, yellow onion, garlic, carrots and parsley. Cook until onions begin to brown. Add the chopped mushroom stems, salt and pepper. Stir occasionally and continue cooking until mushrooms shrink and release their liquid, about five minutes.

Add broth, turn heat to low, cover and let simmer for ten minutes.

For smooth soup (with only rough texture coming from sliced mushroom caps later), pour the cooked mixture through a sieve or cheesecloth (for ultimate smoothness) and discard vegetable chunks.

For chunkier soup, purée vegetables with immersion blender, food processor or stand blender.

Return soup to sauce pot over medium low heat. Add goat cheese and sour cream, stirring occasionally until cream and cheese is melted and incorporated while the soup heats up again.

Add sliced mushroom caps to pot, stir and then cover. Reduce heat to low, reducing heat further if necessary to make sure the soup does not boil. Continue simmering for 20 minutes.

Turn off heat and let sit for a few minutes until it soup is cool enough to eat, adding more salt to taste if needed.

Vegetable Cheese Soup

One day for lunch Big D wanted cheese soup and Little B wanted vegetable soup. We rarely find a canned soup to our liking, much less a wheat free version, so if we want it we make it.

The good news was we keep a fridge full of cheese and vegetables. The bad news was I did not feel like being a short order cook, so I came up with a one pot wonder. Seeing that there were about three spoonfuls of leftovers, I think they did not mind the merger.

- 14-16 ounces broth
- 1 cup beer (I suggest an ale), or additional broth
- 2 cups finely chopped broccoli
- 1 cup finely chopped cauliflower
- 1/2 cup finely chopped carrots
- 1/2 cup finely chopped yellow onion
- 1 plum tomato, finely chopped
- 4 cloves garlic, finely chopped
- 2 cups grated mix of cheddar, Monterrey Jack and mozzarella cheeses
- 1/2 cup heavy whipping cream
- Salt and pepper to taste

In a medium pot over medium high heat add the broth and beer.

When it is starting to boil add the broccoli, cauliflower, carrots, tomato, garlic and onion. Cook for about five minutes, until the vegetables start to soften and soup is hot.

Add 1/2 cup of cheese, stirring until combined and the soup is hot again (after it got cooled off from adding the cheese).

Continue adding and stirring in cheese 1/2 cup at a time and reheating soup in between until it is all incorporated.

Add cream and stir to combine. Cover and let simmer on low for about ten minutes then serve.

1 tablespoon butter or ghee
1 garlic clove, crushed
1/2 small onion, finely chopped
1 small head broccoli, roughly chopped
12 ounces hoppy beer (I suggest India Pale Ale), or substitute 16 ounces chicken broth
2 cups sharp cheddar cheese, grated
1 cup mozzarella cheese, grated
1/2 cup heavy whipping cream
1/4 cup Parmesan cheese (optional)

Broccoli Beer Cheese Soup

A challenge I often have when making a soup with cheese is ensuring the cheese is well combined, and is balanced with the liquid, so it does not become a big cheese glop on the bottom of the pot. I think I found a good balance here. Taking time to gradually add and fully incorporate the cheese, letting the soup heat back up after the cooling effect of the cheese, is the secret.

This soup has a strong flavor because of the strong beer, so if you want a more mild soup, then vary the beer, for it will be your guide. If you do not cook with beer I have suggested a substitute.

In a medium sauce pan combine over medium high heat melt the butter. Add the garlic and onion, cooking until transparent.

Add the broccoli and toss, letting it cook for a minute or two. When the broccoli begins to sweat a bit, about two minutes, add the beer. Bring mixture to a boil and turn down temperature to low. Cover and let simmer for about ten minutes, until onion and broccoli are very soft. Remove from heat and let cool for a few minutes, until it is safe to purée.

With a stand blender or hand blender in the sauce pan, purée liquid and vegetables until all the pieces are very small and uniform. Return mixture to the stove top over medium high heat and make sure it returns to a boil. When hot, gradually add cheddar and mozzarella cheeses, about 1/3 cup at a time, and stir until each portion is completely melted and combined.

After all the cheese is combined, turn down temperature to low and let simmer for about ten minutes, stirring after five minutes. Add the whipping cream and stir some more. If you want the soup smoother, again use the blender to achieve desired smoothness, but remember that it will always be a little bumpy because of the broccoli.

Sprinkle with Parmesan cheese (optional) and serve.

Two Day Chicken Vegetable Soup

When it comes to soup I prefer mine chunky. I also make creamy and puréed soup, but rely on them mostly for first courses or snacks.

A main course soup needs to be chunky in my world. My chicken soup comes with yet another dimension: slow cooked chicken. I have tried to sear the chicken right before adding it to the soup, or steaming it just enough to avoid adding raw meat to the soup, but it just does not work for me. I like chicken in my soup that has the flavor of slow cooked meat.

This chicken soup of mine is a two day process, so don't think you can just throw things in a crock pot one morning and return that evening with dinner ready. No no no. You can return two nights later for dinner.

It is a double crock pot meal, and not because you might happen to own two crock pots. It is a consecutive process, not concurrent. I slow cook the meat one day, prep it, let it rest, then slow cook the soup the next day. It really does taste better. Really.

Day 1

> 6-8 chicken thighs
> 5 cloves garlic
> 1 tablespoon cumin
> 1 10-ounce can Rotel® tomatoes and green chiles*
> Salt and pepper to taste

Season chicken thoroughly by sprinkling it with cumin, salt and pepper. Pour half the can of Rotel® in a 5-quart crock pot. Arrange chicken on top of the Rotel®. Chop garlic and sprinkle on top of chicken, then add the rest of the Rotel®. Cover and cook on high for first two hours, then lower temperature and cook for four more hours. If you are gone for the day it can be cooked on low for eight hours with similar results.

When cooled debone and remove skin from the thighs. Shred meat into bite-size pieces. Retain liquid, including any pieces remaining of the tomatoes and chiles. Store meat and liquid separately overnight in the refrigerator.

If no Rotel® is available you can substitute 3/4 cup diced tomatoes and 1/2 cup green chiles.

Day 2

Chicken meat and liquid from Day 1
5-6 cups water
20 petite carrots, quartered or 2 large carrots, chopped
2 potatoes peeled, halved and sliced thin (replace with 2 cups chopped cabbage if avoiding potatoes)
2 cups peas (exclude if avoiding legumes)
2 cups corn (exclude if avoiding all grains or corn)
1 bunch celery hearts with leaves, chopped
2 cups mixed cauliflower and broccoli, chopped
1 small onion, chopped
1 tablespoon dried thyme
1 tablespoon dried parsley
1 teaspoon ground sage
Salt to taste

Remove chicken meat and liquid from fridge. Skim fat off top of liquid and discard. Pour liquid into the bottom of the crock pot.

Add vegetables and herbs, topping with chicken meat. Stir together all ingredients. Add water until meat and vegetables are just covered with liquid and stir again.

Cover and cook six hours on high or eight hours on low. Turn off heat and taste, adding salt and pepper if desired. Let soup sit for about an hour before serving.

Serve with Power Bread or Cornless Cornbread.

Vegetables

1 large head cauliflower, cut into 1 inch pieces
1/2 cup water
1 teaspoon sea salt
1/2 cup butter or ghee
4 cloves garlic, crushed*
1 tablespoon dried thyme leaves*
Salt to taste

2 tablespoons creamy cheese (cream cheese, goat cheese, herbed cheese, ?) (optional)

Mashed Cauliflower

Mashed cauliflower is a staple of ours that appeases any craving I ever had for mashed potatoes. The flavor and texture are rich and smooth. It is a really easy dish, but the results can vary as far as thickness and smoothness. Over the years we have experimented with ingredients and processes—chopping finely before cooking, steaming the head whole, steaming then using a hand blender to purée, using a potato smasher to get a rough consistency. All of this experimentation led to a wonderful conclusion: cook the cauliflower in chunks with very little water, then purée after draining the steaming liquid—this method seems to give it just the right texture and thickness.

Too thin and you get soup, too thick and the flavors just don't mix the right way. When it is just right—very Goldilocks is what I call it—the dish is addictive and will do you proud on any holiday dinner table. Don't get me wrong, the soupy version and the one with flavors not mixing just right are delicious as well, but we challenge ourselves to get dishes-just-right.

The following version is wonderfully thick, but not too thick, and flavorful. It definitely has a place of honor on our table. It is a dish that really is better the next day, so take advantage of that fact and make it the day before, only needing a quick heating up before serving.

In a large pot add water and 1 teaspoon salt. Bring to a boil and add cauliflower. Lower temperature and cover, steaming until soft, about 10 minutes.

Place cauliflower in food processor or blender, retaining liquid from pot, and purée until smooth. When smooth, return cauliflower to the pot and add butter, garlic and thyme. Turn heat on under pan to low and cook until butter is melted and spices are blended. It should be the consistency of natural peanut butter—not stiff but not runny.

If you are adding creamy cheese fold it in now and stir occasionally until it is melted and combined. The cheese can also be added when the cauliflower is reheated instead.

The cauliflower can be served immediately, or chilled overnight to maximize the blending of flavors. Reheat over low heat on stove top for best results, but microwaving on 50% power, stirring every five minutes until hot, works as well.

Quantities of garlic and thyme allow for clearly tasting both flavors. Reduce amounts if a more subtle flavor of one or the other is preferred.

- 3 tablespoons butter or ghee
- 1 large head cauliflower
- 1 tablespoon ground turmeric
- 1 teaspoon sea salt
- 1 teaspoon ground ginger
- 2 teaspoons garlic powder
- 1 teaspoon onion powder
- 1/4 cup heavy whipping cream

Yellow Mashed Cauliflower (Yellaflower)

Turmeric is an entertaining ingredient to use. It turns everything it touches a brilliant shade of orange-yellow, so it is sometimes hard to keep the kitchen un-yellow. Be it my hands, the counter, spatula or the food itself, there is no doubt when it was used.

When combining turmeric with the sometimes drab color of cauliflower, it cannot help but brighten up any plate. Big D loves turmeric, and we both take it as a daily anti-inflammatory supplement, so I pulled out our big container of the powder and added some to our lunch's steamed and seared cauliflower side dish.

Little B came through and asked what was for lunch. When I mentioned steamed cauliflower she excitedly asked if it was going to be mashed...why not?! It was mushed instead of left whole. Our traditional mashed cauli is great, but this yellaflower is quite flavorful and gave wonderful balance to the tomato sauce and cheesy meatballs I served on top of it.

Cut cauliflower into chunky pieces. In a medium stock pot over medium heat melt the butter. Add the cauliflower and cover. Stir occasionally until the florets begin to release liquid, about five minutes.

Sprinkle with turmeric, salt, ginger, garlic and onion, tossing until the spices coat the florets. Lower temperature and cover, cooking until cauliflower is soft, about five more minutes.

Purée the cauliflower and whipping cream either in the pot with an immersion blender, or by placing the cauliflower and cream in a food processor. The end product should be thick, smooth and bright yellow.

Serve immediately in place of rice, polenta, pasta, or as a side dish.

2 pounds fresh broccoli florets
1 pound fresh cauliflower florets
1/2 small onion, diced
1/2 cup butter, sliced into eight pieces, or ghee
2 teaspoons dried thyme leaves
3 cloves garlic, crushed
1 teaspoon sea salt

Broccoli Cauliflower Mash

If you are looking for a quick, different, single pot side dish then your search is over. It really stands out from the ones that leave the vegetables all whole and overly recognizable! I first got the idea for this dish from my mother in law. We started making straight mashed cauliflower a few years ago, and I would like to think that it was contagious, eventually creeping into the kitchen of the in-laws. During one of our visits to Texas this broccoli cauliflower mash appeared and was delicious!

I don't know exactly what she put in her dish for seasoning, but I did ours the way we like it—buttery with a little help from garlic and thyme. When I first saw it sitting on my plate it reminded me of mushed peas. When I put it in my mouth it was definitely not made of peas. The mash was light, dreamy, and very much complemented the tender smoked salmon Big D cooked up. A weeknight dinner was on the table in no time!

In a medium pot pour 1 cup water and add broccoli, cauliflower and onion. Cook over medium-high heat until vegetables are soft, 8-10 minutes. Drain and retain water from pot.

Add thyme, garlic, salt, and butter slices, stirring until mostly melted. Using an immersion stick blender, purée until vegetables are smooth. If purée is too thick for your taste add a small amount of the water retained from boiling the vegetables to thin it out.

Mash can be served immediately, but flavors will combine more thoroughly after resting for an hour or more.

Cauliflower Mac Bake

This dish definitely appeased my craving for baked mac and cheese (not so much the boxed version I grew up eating, but the robust, baked stuff I discovered later in life). The dish was easy to prepare and bake, allowing me to time it perfectly with the smoked pork Big D made. Add some chimichurri to the pork and what a meal!

- 1 large head cauliflower
- 1/2 cup heavy cream
- 2 eggs
- 1 tablespoon parsley, finely chopped
- 1/2 teaspoon garlic powder
- 1/2 teaspoon sea salt
- 1 teaspoon ground mustard
- 1/2 teaspoon red chili flakes
- 2 cups cheddar cheese, grated
- 1/4 pound sharp white cheddar cheese, sliced into thin pieces
- 3 tablespoons butter

Preheat oven to 350 degrees.

Chop cauliflower head into bite-sized pieces, making sure stem pieces are a little smaller. Place white cheddar cheeses slices in the bottom of a 9x9 or 9-11 baking dish. Spread cauliflower evenly over cheese.

In a medium bowl combine cream, eggs, garlic, salt, mustard and chili flakes. Whisk until well combined. Add cheese and stir until well combined. Pour cheese mixture over cauliflower, spreading it evenly.

Make thin slices of the butter and place them on top of cheese mixture. Place in preheated oven for 60-75 minutes. The larger the cauliflower pieces the longer the baking time needed to make sure the middle pieces are soft.

Remove from oven and let sit for five minutes before serving. Slice into six sections for main dish or nine pieces for side dish portions.

1/2 large head cauliflower
2 whole eggs
1/4 cup golden flaxseed meal
1/4 cup fresh parsley, finely chopped
1 teaspoon lime juice
1/2 teaspoon salt
1/4 teaspoon black pepper
1 teaspoon fresh thyme
1/2 teaspoon ground cinnamon
1/4 teaspoon chili powder
1/2 teaspoon cumin
1/2 teaspoon tumeric
pinch cayenne pepper
1/2 cup olive oil or fat of your liking

CAULIFLOWER FRITTERS

When I make it a point to avoid processed grains and starchy carbohydrates in my diet I seem to have more energy and lose weight. I also start to crave vegetables. Ideally I would crave steamed veggies with some lime juice and herbs, but the reality is I want usually want more substance, texture and flavor.

These fritters help me balance the need for hearty high fiber veggie variety and a low carb energy source in the flaxseed.

Cut cauliflower into small florets and add to the bowl of your food processor. Process on pulse until cauliflower has a rough texture.

In a large mixing bowl add the rest of the ingredients, except the oil, and mix until well combined. Add the cauliflower and combine until well coated.

Heat a splash of olive oil in a frying pan and add about 1/4 cup of the mixture for each fritter.

Cook three or four fritters at a time for 2–3 minutes on each side, until golden brown, then keep warm (on the stove top or in the oven) while you cook the remaining fritters.

2 tablespoons butter
1 tablespoon coconut flour
1 teaspoon salt
1/4 cup onion, diced
2 cups mushrooms, diced
1 cup sour cream
1 tablespoon Worchestershire sauce (soy free)
3 cans French style green beans, drained
2 cups shredded Cheddar cheese

Soupless Green Bean Casserole

I like holiday meals. Partly because of all the lovely foods we don't make during other times of the year, but also because the meals often require cooking all day. We like spending time in the kitchen. It is a place where we have great conversation and create or try new dishes. This is a good thing, in my opinion.

Besides a huge bird or a massive ham, I always look forward to green bean casserole. There is something about the beans and the creamy sauce and the occasional mushroom bits all swirled together in a single bite. This version of the casserole does not include the crunchy fried onions, because of the wheaty carbiness of them, but it still turned out to appease my comfort food craving for the soupy, crunchy version.

This recipe should also work well with whole fresh beans if prepared properly, but with the canned French style the sauce coated every bit very well and the richness I love so much was able to shine through. I am not partial to all the extra junk they put in canned soups, as I have ranted about before, so I am always glad to figure out versions of comfort foods I enjoy without the processed stuff.

Preheat oven to 350F.
Melt 2 tablespoons butter in a large skillet over medium heat. Stir in coconut flour until smooth, and cook for one minute. Stir in the salt, onion, Worcestershire sauce and sour cream.
Add mushrooms. Cook mixture until mushrooms sweat and liquid reduces by half.
Add green beans, and stir to coat and heat.
Transfer the mixture to a 9x9 casserole dish. Spread shredded cheese over the top. Bake for 30 minutes, or until the top is golden and cheese is bubbly.

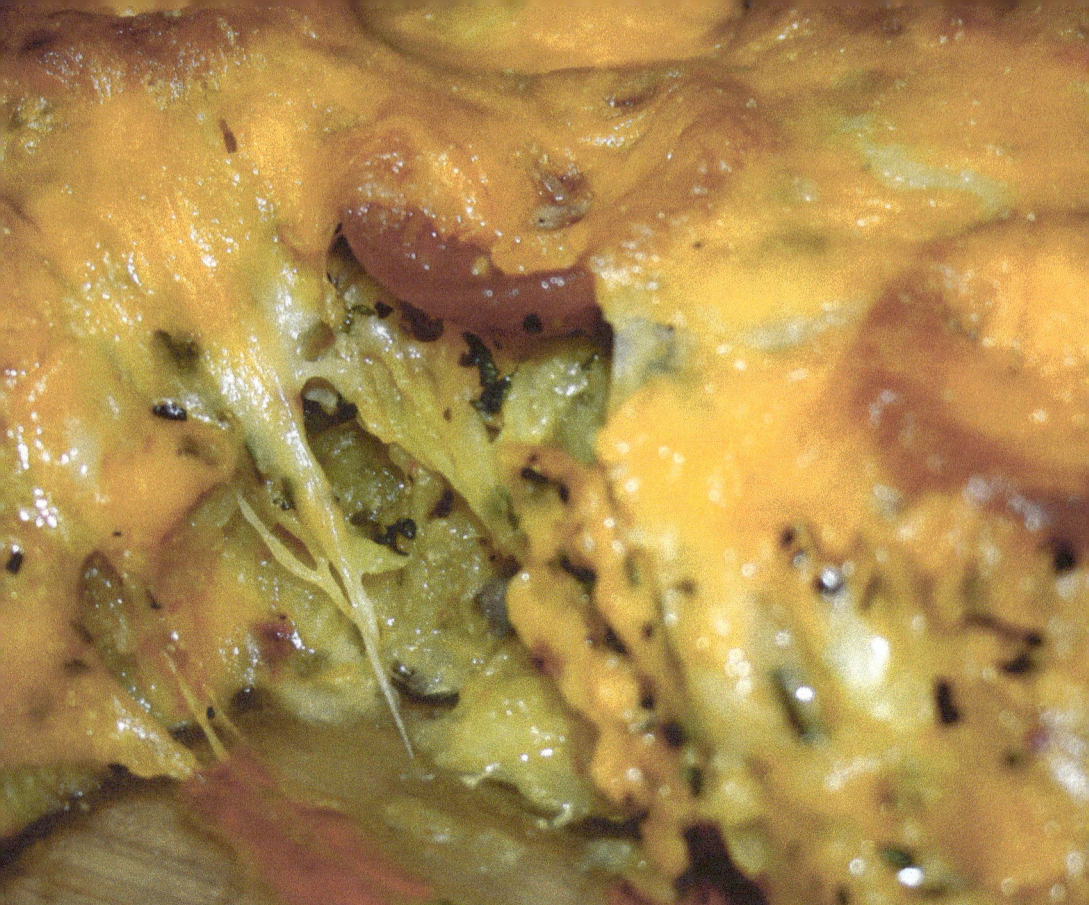

1 large spaghetti squash
8-12 ounces pepperoni, sliced thick
2 cups shredded cheddar cheese
2 cups Italian mix cheese (Romano, mozzarella, Parmesan...)
2 cups roughly chopped mushrooms (or 8 ounces canned mushrooms)
2 tablespoons dried parsley
2 tablespoons dried oregano
2 teaspoons dried basil
2 teaspoons garlic powder
2-3 teaspoons sea salt
2 teaspoons red pepper flakes
1 teaspoon black pepper

Spaghetti Squash Pizza Bake

We love pizza and we love squash, especially spaghetti squash. It is a great way to take care of those pizza cravings, because the wheaty crust of the traditional pizza is just not gonna work with our diet strategy.

Yes you need a fork to eat it, but is it really a great loss? If you are watching your carbohydrate intake like me, there is nothing better for battling pizza advertisements. The squash does a wonderful job of helping the herbs mix and spread their joy, and thick sliced pepperoni is just heaven to me on a pizza.

Slice squash in half lengthwise and scrape out seeds and sinew. In a microwave safe dish place halves open side down and add about 1/2 cup water. Cook on high for 10-12 minutes. If you cook one half at a time the cooking time is about 8 minutes. Remove from oven and let cool.

Preheat the oven to 350 Fahrenheit.

While the squash cools prepare the rest of the dish—start with slicing pepperoni and roughly chopping mushrooms.

When squash is cooled scrape out the 'spaghetti' with a fork into a bowl.

Add mushrooms to the squash along with half of the herbs, salt and pepper and toss thoroughly.

In a medium to large rectangular baking dish (no larger than 9x13) sprinkle about 1/2 cup of the cheddar cheese. Add the squash mixture. Take a mix of the cheese, about a cup, and spread on top of the squash mixture, pushing it into the squash a bit. Add the rest of the herbs and spices.

Make a layer of the pepperoni, then top with the remaining cheese.

Place in preheated oven and cook for 30-35 minutes, until cheese is melted and there is some browning.

Let stand outside the oven for about ten minutes before serving.

Slice like a casserole and serve with a simple garden salad.

1 spaghetti squash
1 tablespoon extra virgin olive oil
Salt to taste
1 teaspoon garlic powder
1/2-1 cup mozzarella cheese, grated
1/4-1/2 cup Parmesan cheese, grated
1 teaspoon dried oregano
2 teaspoons dried parsley

Baked Cheese And Herb Spaghetti Squash

This stuff is just plain cute. Besides being yummy, serving it in the squash skin makes it fun to eat! I remember when I first had spaghetti squash. My mom served it under a red marinara sauce and said it was just like pasta. That caused the problem—unintended, but problematic. I expected some slight mushiness that started to soak up the sauce, like real pasta. What I got was slightly crunchy strings that mixed with the sauce, but did not absorb. I did not find it appealing after the first encounter.

Flash forward a few years. I tried spaghetti squash again, with the expectation of squash, not pasta. It tasted lovely, absorbing the garlic and herbs tossed with it, instead of futilely attempting to soak up marinara. You should try it too!

Preheat oven to 375 degrees.

Cut squash in half lengthwise and remove seeds. Drizzle olive oil on the halves and use your hands to spread it all over the exposed meat of the squash. Place halves face down on baking sheet. Bake for 30-45 minutes until inside of squash is soft, but not mushy.

Reduce oven temperature to 350 degrees.

Flip over squash halves, carefully hold the hot squash with a mitt or towel. Using a fork, scrape the squash meat off the skin, but leave it in the shell. Sprinkle the squash with salt and garlic powder, then gently toss the meat within the skin. Sprinkle with a little more salt. Divide mozzarella and sprinkle on each half, followed by the oregano and parsley. Finish with sprinkling the Parmesan cheese on top.

Return squash to oven on baking sheet, cheese side up. Bake for 15-20 minutes, until cheese is melted and beginning to brown.

Remove from oven and serve immediately—small squash can result in an entire half being a side dish, while larger squash may need to be cut into quarters for serving.

2 large, narrow zucchini
2 14-ounce cans diced tomatoes
1 small can tomato paste
2 teaspoons dried oregano leaves
2 teaspoons dried parsley leaves
2 cloves garlic, crushed
1/2 teaspoon salt
1/8 teaspoon pure stevia powder (equivalent to 2 teaspoons pure cane sugar)
12-15 ounces ricotta cheese
2 cups fresh baby spinach leaves, finely chopped
1 teaspoon ground nutmeg
1 egg
1 1/2 pounds ground Italian sausage, cooked thoroughly and crumbled
1 cup sliced mushrooms
4 cups mozzarella cheese

Zucchini Lasagna

When I make this lasagna I do not really feel like I missed out on pasta, even after we spent some time in Italy. There were almost as many places in the lovely country to get a skewer of roasted meat as there were pizza slices, so our efforts to watch our carbs on the trip were not as difficult as we thought.

The time we spent renting a villa in Tuscany was sprinkled with visits to the local co-op for freshly butchered meat and freshly picked produce. The cheeses and cured meats were quite an experience, too.

Of course, the evil alcoholic concoction we came up with while relaxing the nights away made the eating at the villa a pleasant blur. We would take Coca-Cola Light (the Italian version of diet Coke) and mix it with some quite horrible tasting Grappa. We did find what I consider very good Grappa before we left, but that first bottle was nasty. Not to waste alcohol, we combined it with the soda and boom! We dubbed our creation Crappa. We proceeded to get schnockered and did some skinny dipping in the pool.

To make a long story short, and totally disconnected to our libation, this recipe takes care of my lasagna craving while keeping me away from the processed carbs found in the pasta part of the dish.

Preheat oven to 350F.

In small sauce pan combine the diced tomatoes, paste, oregano, parsley, onion powder, salt, and stevia. Bring to a boil over medium heat, turn down flame and simmer for about 15 minutes, then remove from flame and set aside.

While sauce is cooking prepare the rest of the dish. In a medium bowl mix the ricotta cheese, egg, spinach, and nutmeg and set aside—trust me—it sounds odd, but the nutmeg enhances the ricotta flavor.

Slice ends off of zucchini. With a vegetable peeler peel off long strips of zucchini. If you don't have a peeler, instead make zucchini coins as thin as you can with a knife.

To build the lasagna begin with a thin layer of sauce in the bottom of a 9x13-inch baking dish.

Add zucchini strips/coins overlapping generously to make a solid layer, followed by the ricotta mixture, sauce, mushrooms, sausage and 1 cup of mozzarella. Repeat the layers again. Top with a third layer of zucchini and the last of the mozzarella.

Bake lasagna until heated through and cheese on top begins to brown, about 45 minutes. Remove from oven and let cool for about ten minutes, allowing the lasagna to set.

1 tablespoon extra virgin olive oil
1/2 yellow onion, julienned
2 garlic cloves, chopped
1 yellow squash
1 zucchini
Sea salt and ground black pepper to taste

Sauteed Squash Strings

If a kitchen gadget cannot be used for three or more different purposes I am hard pressed to acquire or keep it. Things like avocado slicers, cherry pitters, cheese slicers, and the like are not found in our kitchen drawers. On the other hand, our thirteen-year-old Wusthof knife set goes with us everywhere.

One thing I have not been able to do consistently without a gadget is make vegetable 'noodles.' I can use a vegetable peeler to make strips of veggies (yes, the peeler always makes the cut), but not so much the thicker or rounder noodles I want as a base.

I caved and finally bought one of those twisty vegetable noodle makers. It works well and is compact (I bought the smaller, non-deluxe version). I have used the noodles under sauces in place of pasta, used them as a side dish, and even as part of tacos and enchiladas, which I must say went especially well. Using the gadget reminds me of peeling oranges as a child—I always tried to peel them in one long strip. This gadget can literally make one long noodle out of a zucchini. The problem with a three-foot-long noodle is dividing it among diners, so ponder some trimming either before or after cooking.

I use them as a conduit to compliment other foods, like other people use rice or pasta, so keeping the preparation simple makes so much sense. When you make them to complement another part of your meal, play around with the herbs and spices, but for a standard dish, the onion and garlic are always a good place to start.

Twist zucchini and yellow squash through thick setting of a vegetable noodle gadget, placing 'noodles' into a bowl. With a sharp knife cut an X through the noodles, allowing for shorter, bite-sized strips.

In a medium skillet over medium high heat add oil. When oil is hot add garlic and onion. Cook until onion begins to brown on edges. Lower heat to medium.

Add squash strips to pan and season with salt and pepper. Toss squash with onion and garlic until heated through, but stop before squash begins to go limp and release liquid, about two minutes.

Remove from pan and serve immediately, either as a side dish, taco filler or 'pasta' under sauce.

Baked Zucchini Wedges

I did it! I finally did it! I made a zucchini dish that Big D declared as the best he has ever had. This is a BIG deal. I love zucchini, but Big D does not. As usual, if I cover something with garlic and cheese there is a high possibility of culinary success around here. These are delicious hot or cold.

I don't know if this bread-crumb-less version will work with anything other than the powdery Parmesan cheese typically found in shaker-type containers, but I do know the powdery stuff did a great job of sticking, with the help of some egg.

- 2 large zucchini
- 2 cups finely grated Parmesan cheese (make sure it is real cheese!)
- 2 teaspoons garlic powder
- 1 teaspoon salt
- 2 eggs
- 2 tablespoons water

Preheat oven to 350 degrees. Prepare a large non-stick cookie sheet to receive the coated slices.

Slice zucchini in half width-wise, then lengthwise into narrow wedges—at least 20 slices per squash.

Mix together eggs and water, making sure they are well combined. Whisk it quickly if you need to. Pour into a shallow bowl or deep plate.

In another bowl/plate combine cheese, garlic and salt.

Dip each slice into the egg mixture, followed by dipping in the cheese mixture. If they will stand on their skin edge, then set them on the sheet skin side down. If they only stand on a wide, white edge, they will be fine, but will cook darker brown on the side touching the pan.

Bake for about 30 minutes until coating on top starts browning. Serve immediately.

2 acorn squash
3 tablespoons olive oil
1 teaspoon cinnamon
1 teaspoon salt

Roasted Acorn Squash

This roasted version of acorn squash has three advantages: 1) it makes the squash almost finger food, which gets more inside of Little B, 2) the skin is soft enough to eat along with the flesh, and adds more nutritional value to the dish, and 3) it adds a bit of natural sweetness to an otherwise savory meal.

Preheat oven to 400 degrees.

Cut squash in half lengthwise and remove stringy membrane and seeds, then horizontally make slices about 1/2 inch wide to create "C" shaped pieces.

Grease a large cookie sheet with 1 tablespoon of the olive oil. Place squash pieces on sheet in one layer.

Sprinkle remaining oil on top of slices. The best way to evenly distribute the oil is to get messy—pour it on your hands and wipe the top of each piece with your oiled fingers.

Sprinkle slices with cinnamon and salt.

Bake in oven for about 25 minutes, until squash is tender (a fork slides easily into the thicker pieces) and just starting to turn golden brown. Do not be deceived—it may not look done, but it really will be. Serve immediately.

4 large portobello mushrooms, stems removed
1 tablespoon lime juice
1/2 cup tomato paste
2 teaspoons dried oregano leaves
2 teaspoons dried parsley leaves
2 teaspoons dried basil leaves
2 teaspoons garlic powder
8 ounces pepperoni, sliced thick
2 cups grated mozzarella cheese
1/2 cup Parmesan cheese
Salt and pepper to taste

Portobello Pizzas

The first time I ever cooked with portobello mushrooms was about 15 years ago. At the time I was making a lot of pizzas closely following my discovery of pizza stones. The stones make the crust crispy all around and are great for getting an evenly cooked result. I got into the habit of topping each pizza with two to three veggies and a meat. On some occasions my dinner guests were vegetarians, so minus the meat, but what to add to make the pizza hearty? I explored the produce section of the grocery store and came upon the portobellos—huge caps sitting over a sign that described them as meaty. Well, why not? If they don't eat meat, why not serve them meaty mushrooms? The pizza with portobellos turned out great, and marinating the mushrooms added an extra layer of flavor.

One recent tendency has been to make pizzas with low carb crust, and another is to reach back into my pizza past and snatch up the portobellos and use them as the crust. They are quick and of course Little B can help with every step. Using tomato paste adds a spike of tomato flavor without adding much liquid. The one flaw, but not really, in this recipe is the inevitable wetness of the mushrooms. When cooked they 'sweat,' so unless you burn the dickens out of them, you will never have dry portobello pizzas!

Preheat oven to 350 degrees.
Place caps stem side up on baking sheet, then sprinkle with lime juice, salt and pepper.
Spread tomato paste on mushrooms, followed by a layer of basil, oregano, parsley, and basil leaves, along with garlic powder.
Place a layer of pepperoni slices and top with mozzarella and Parmesan cheeses.
Bake for 20-25 minutes, until mushrooms are tender and cheese is melted and browning.

4 small or 3 medium russet potatoes
2 tablespoons avocado or extra virgin olive oil
1 teaspoon salt
1 teaspoon garlic powder
Dash of pepper

CRISPY BAKED CHIPS

You want fries with that? Of course, but I shouldn't...

These baked fries cook up so crispy, and the seasoning begs not to be dipped in anything. These are chips, as in fish 'n chips! These little guys taste like they could have been deep fried, but they are baked, much lower fat than their deep-fried counterparts, crispy and addictive!

Wash and slice potatoes into thin wedges lengthwise, approximately 12 per potato.

Soak slices in a bowl of cold water for 10 minutes.

Preheat oven to 425 degrees.

Lay out wedges on a towel to dry, pressing down from above using another towel to get as much water off as possible.

Place wedges in a bowl and sprinkle with oil, salt, pepper and garlic, tossing until completely coated.

Spread wedges out in one layer on large cookie sheet, skin down, or if placed on a cut edge, they will have to be flipped during baking. Bake in oven for about 20 minutes.

Flip wedges over if baking on their sides, or rotate pan 180 degrees to ensure even baking if sitting on their skins, and return to oven for 10-20 minutes.

The second baking time varies so much because the size of the wedges may vary. By the time the first bake time is over the potatoes will be cooked—the second time is to ensure complete and utter crispiness.

Serve immediately.

NOTE: The recipe can be easily doubled. Just make sure you have sufficient baking sheet space. If doubling the recipe and cooking on two sheets, which probably means using two levels of the stove, you will need to cook them twenty minutes, then switch levels the sheets are on for the additional time to allow for even browning.

Jicama Fries

In my opinion jicama is crispy and a bit sweet, and more flavorful than the traditional potato used for fries. The big piles we made were eaten up by the three of us and our visiting family, so I cannot speak to the robustness of leftovers.

- 1 jicama
- 1 tablespoon avocado oil
- 1/4 cup Parmesan cheese, finely grated
- 1/4 teaspoon garlic powder
- 1/4 teaspoon onion powder
- 1/4 teaspoon sea salt

Preheat oven to 350 degrees.

Peel jicama. Slice it into disks no thicker than 1/4 inch. Slice disks into French fry shaped sticks.

In a large bowl toss fries with the avocado oil. In a plastic bag combine cheese, garlic, onion and salt. Add fries and shake until coated.

Place fries evenly spaced on a baking sheet, for too little space in between can prevent crisping. Depending on the size of the pan and the jicama, you may need two or more pans. Bake for 15 minutes. Remove from oven and flip the fries.

If you are baking with two pans make sure you switch their position in the oven—my oven bakes faster on the bottom rack if there are two in at the same time, so switching after tossing helps them all cook evenly.

Return to oven and bake for 10-15 minutes more, until edges are crispy and brown. Serve immediately.

- 4 cups shredded green cabbage
- 1 cup shredded purple cabbage (or additional green cabbage)
- 1/2 cup shredded carrot (optional)
- 1/2 cup finely chopped red onion
- 1 clove garlic, crushed
- 1 cup mayonnaise
- 1/4 cup apple cider vinegar
- 1 teaspoon sea salt
- 1/2 teaspoon ground black pepper

Coleslaw

Big D and I used to have a serious issue. I like tart coleslaw and he likes slightly sweet coleslaw. It makes for a challenge when making, well, coleslaw. I could make two batches, but that seems silly, so I just kept experimenting until I figured out a just-right combination of sweet and tart in one bowl of slaw.

I previously tried to use sweetener and white or wine vinegar to get a balance, but then had a revelation and tried—duh—a different kind of vinegar. The apple cider vinegar has just enough sweet and tart to get to the balance we like. Voilà! The perfect coleslaw.

In a large bowl combine garlic, mayonnaise, vinegar, salt, and pepper. Whisk until combined.

Add green cabbage, purple cabbage, carrot, and onion. Toss vegetables until coated with dressing. Chill for at least one hour before serving.

Chicken

8 chicken thighs, with bone and skin
2 chicken breasts, with bone and skin
1/2 cup butter or other fat, melted
2 bags pork rinds
1 cup grated Parmesan cheese (make sure it is real cheese!)
1/4 cup parsley, finely chopped
1 tablespoon garlic powder
2 teaspoons onion powder
2 teaspoons cumin powder
2 teaspoons sea salt
1 teaspoon ground black pepper
1 tablespoon dried oregano leaves

Crispy Baked Chicken

I have seen the use of crushed pork rinds as a 'breading' in a lot of different places lately. I was originally going to use the approach to breading we rely on for Scotch Eggs, using golden flaxseed meal, but wanted to try the pork rind approach first.

We are usually dark chicken meat people, but had house guests that preferred white meat, so we caved in and made it too. Adding the variety gave us an opportunity to try three different chicken conditions—dark meat, larger breasts of white meat, and skinless 'tenders.' The results were awesome—the pork rind breading worked on everything! Leftovers were a little soggy when microwaved instead of toasted/baked, but straight out of the oven worked for me as a fried chicken replacement.

Preheat oven to 350 degrees. Line shallow baking sheets with aluminum foil.

Using a blender or food processor cut the pork rinds into small crumbs. Place crumbs in large mixing bowl. Add cheese and spices to the crumbs and stir until combined.

Remove bones from chicken breasts while leaving the skin attached, removing separately the long tenderloin pieces along the bone for 'chicken strips.' Slice chicken breasts in half, making four evenly sized pieces. Season all sides of all pieces of chicken with sea salt.

One at a time coat each piece of chicken with butter, then thoroughly coat all surfaces of each one with the crumb mixture. Place each piece, skin side up, on the baking sheets, leaving about an inch of space around each piece. Bake for about one hour, until juices run clear.

Serve immediately.

3 pounds wing pieces, frozen or thawed
1 tablespoon apple cider vinegar
2 tablespoons yellow mustard
1 tablespoon lime juice
1/2 cup finely grated Parmesan cheese
1/2 teaspoon ground turmeric
1 tablespoon dried parsley flakes
1 teaspoon sea salt
1 teaspoon ground black pepper
2 teaspoons ground garlic powder
1 teaspoon ground onion powder
2 teaspoons red pepper flakes (optional)

Mustard Parmesan Wings

I have a love and loathing relationship with my kitchen. It has nothing to do with whether or not I enjoy cooking, it is just that I don't always want to cook. What is worse, I think Big D is very similar. There is not always the desire to do, but there is often the desire to eat. Since we rarely bring home prepared or processed foods, there is a constant need to make food with the wonderful ingredients we bring into our home. In finding a balance between needing to eat and wanting to cook I have come up with numerous recipes that don't take much prep time.

Here is a quick dinner that comes in handy, especially for my wing loving self. The great part about this recipe is that it completely comes from our freezer and pantry, full of staples we always have around. No excuses for not eating well if your pantry is stocked!

Preheat oven to 375 degrees.

Line two small or one large shallow aluminum baking sheet(s) with aluminum foil.

In large bowl combine all ingredients except chicken. Stir to combine.

Add chicken and stir until chicken is coated (either with a wooden spoon or hands). Place chicken in one layer on baking sheet. If the chicken is frozen the coating may not stick as well, so you may need to spread it on chicken after placing pieces on baking sheets.

Place in oven and bake for 45-60 minutes, until juices running from chicken are clear.

Remove from oven and let sit for five minutes before serving. May be dipped in the sauce/dressing of your choice, but are wonderful without.

3 pounds boneless skinless chicken pieces
  (tenders and thighs recommended)
2 pounds raw pecans
1 teaspoon sea salt
1 teaspoon garlic powder
3 egg whites
2 tablespoons Dijon mustard
Sea salt and ground black pepper to taste

Pecan Crusted Chicken

It is amazingly difficult to avoid wheat in convenience foods at stores and restaurants in America. Take a quick look at kid menus in quick serve and sit-down service restaurants—you are most likely to see choices like burgers, grilled cheese sandwiches, corn dogs, macaroni and cheese, and some sort of breaded chicken. Most often included are the lovely and mysterious chicken nuggets and tenders—lovely because they are often crispy and mysterious because it not always clear what parts of the chicken are tendered or nuggetted.

The pecan version of tenders presented below sure fit the bill of finger food or dippable chicken. The nuts chop up into various sizes, adding a nice texture which mixes well with the chicken. Little B eats them plain, but I like dipping in dressing or mustard.

They are filling too—instead of feeling hungry soon after eating nuggets coated with wheat, the nut coating fills me up fast and keeps me full for a while.

Preheat oven to 400 degrees.

In a food processor pulse pecans, salt, and garlic powder until nuts are finely chopped.

In a medium bowl whisk together egg whites and mustard until well combined, but stop short of the whites becoming stiff.

Line one large or two small shallow baking sheets with aluminum foil.

Spread the nuts on a third sheet or large plate. Generously season chicken with salt and pepper.

Dip the chicken in the egg wash, letting the excess run off.

Roll chicken in the nuts, gently pressing them into the meat.

Place chicken on the foil lined baking sheets with about an inch between pieces.

Bake for 35-45 minutes, until juices run clear (whole chicken breasts or bone-in chicken may take longer).

Serve immediately, plain or with desired dipping sauces.

Chicken Faux Fried Rice

As I continue to explore the many and varied uses of cauliflower, I did some research about using it instead of rice. In the end, using it as a rice substitute, especially in a fried rice type dish, is a lot faster than using traditional rice. The sauté part of this one-dish wonder is just enough time to cook it and keep it at a firmness similar to rice. The cauliflower, combined with using coconut aminos in lieu of soy sauce, made this dish fun to prepare and eat.

1 large head cauliflower
2 pounds skinless, boneless chicken thighs
1 tablespoon ground ginger
1 teaspoon ground mustard
3/4 cup coconut aminos
1 tablespoon coconut oil
4 garlic cloves, crushed
1/2 medium white onion, finely chopped
1 stalk celery
3 eggs, whisked
2 cups mini portobello mushrooms, roughly chopped
2 cups fresh spinach, finely chopped
1 cup mixed vegetables (optional)
Salt and pepper to taste

Cut chicken into small, bite-sized pieces.
In a medium bowl place 1/2 cup coconut aminos, ground mustard, and ground ginger. Whisk together, then add half the mixture to the chicken, making sure it is coated. Place in refrigerator to marinate for about 30 minutes.
Cut cauliflower into pieces small enough to fit in food processor. Fill processor with cauliflower and pulse until at least 3/4 of it is the size of rice grains—having some slightly larger pieces remaining is fine, for they will break down a bit during the cooking process. When all the cauliflower is chopped set it aside.
Cut celery into rough pieces and pulse in processor until very fine, almost a paste.
Pull the chicken from the fridge and separate the chicken

from the marinade, discarding the liquid. Add the chicken to the pan and toss until cooked through, about five minutes for small pieces.

In a large skillet or wok over medium high heat add the coconut oil. When hot add the celery, garlic, and onion. Toss in the oil until it all begins to brown. Add the cauliflower to the pan, turning up the heat slightly to make sure the cauliflower sears. Toss the whole mixture every minute for five minutes. Add mixed vegetables if you are including them.

In a bowl stir together the egg and remaining 1/4 cup coconut aminos. Make a 'bowl' in the middle of the skillet/wok, all the way to the bottom. Pour the egg mixture into the skillet and let it cook for a few seconds. Start stirring it with the chicken and cauliflower mixture until it is all coated. Continue tossing the pan contents until the egg is no longer runny.

Add the spinach and toss, letting everything cook for another minute until the spinach starts to wilt.

Serve immediately with salt, pepper and more coconut aminos as desired.

Beef

3-4 pound beef chuck roast
1 medium yellow onion, roughly chopped
1/2 large head green cabbage, roughly chopped
6-8 ounces tomato paste
2 cups water
1 tablespoon garlic powder
1 tablespoon onion powder
2 tablespoons dried parsley leaves
1 tablespoon dried thyme leaves
2 teaspoons cumin powder
2 teaspoons sea salt
1 tablespoon paprika

Rootless Pot Roast

Pot roast without carrots and potatoes? Well, yeah. I wanted to make a pot roast but without the added carbohydrates from carrots and potatoes. I could cook it all together then not eat the root vegetables, but they would be so sad, and so would I. Instead I added cabbage and onion to soak up the zesty flavors and complement the meat. Of course, after so much cooking time the roast was falling apart and the vegetables were almost dissolved. Darn. It made for a rich, smooth sauce with a hint of veggies.

Some gently steamed lime infused broccoli on the side worked wonders and loved the sauce. As my grade school companions would say, KISS—Keep It Simple, Stupid. Always a good, yet slightly crude and blunt piece of advice.

In a medium bowl combine tomato paste and water. Stir until paste is dissolved. Add all the spices and continue stirring until combined. It will actually thicken.

In a crock pot add a layer of vegetables using half the onion and cabbage. Add the roast and pour the sauce on top. Sprinkle the rest of the vegetables over the roast.

Cover and cook on high for 5-7 hours or on low for about 10 hours. Turn off heat and let sit for about 30 minutes before serving.

For the Stew

    2 tablespoons butter or ghee
    1 pound stew beef or lamb, ground or cut into small bite-sized pieces
    1/2-1 cup red wine
    2 tablespoons tomato paste
    2 cloves garlic, crushed
    2 tablespoons soy free Worcestershire sauce
    1 cup chopped carrots
    1 small onion, chopped
    1 cup frozen peas
    1 cup frozen corn (exclude for a fully grain free dish)

For the Topping

    1 medium head of cauliflower
    2 tablespoons heavy cream
    2 tablespoons butter
    1/2 cup plus 1 cup shredded sharp cheddar cheese
    4 egg whites
    Salt & pepper to taste

Shepherd's Pie With Mashed Cauliflower

The Shepherd's Pie is a dish that has Irish roots much closer than the corned beef commonly eaten in America, especially in March. Here is a version that is very Americanized, or more accurately low carb-ized, for it has not a speck of potato, but as with other manipulations that can be done with cauliflower, you might not miss the 'taters.

This dish is usually called Cottage Pie when beef is used, and Shepherd's Pie when lamb is used. I used ground lamb, so I at least kept to some traditional aspects, even if the top is from a cauliflower patch!

TOPPING: Clean and trim cauliflower, adding florets to a microwave safe bowl with 1/4 cup water. Cover with cling wrap or a vented cover and microwave for 5-8 minutes until soft. Drain water.

Add the cream and butter to the cauliflower bowl and toss until butter is melted. Add the buttered and creamy cauliflower and 1/2 cup of cheese to a food processor or use a hand blender to process until the mixture is a smooth consistency. It should look like thick mashed potatoes. Season with salt and pepper. Let cool to at least room temperature.

Preheat oven to 375 degrees.

STEW: In a skillet over medium high heat melt the butter, then add the meat. Sauté until browned, about five minutes. If an overwhelming amount of liquid and fat is in the meat (if it is pooling in the pan), partially drain and continue cooking. Add red wine and cook until sauce bubbles.

Add tomato paste, garlic, and Worcestershire sauce, stirring until blended. Add onion, corn, and peas. Cover and let simmer for 30 minutes over low heat. Turn off heat and set aside while you finish the topping.

FINISH TOPPING: Right before putting the room temperature cauliflower on top of the meat filling, whisk the egg whites to a stiff peak. Fold 1/3 of the egg whites into the cauliflower mixture to lighten it up. Then fold the remaining egg whites into the cauliflower mixture and gently mix until combined.

In a 9x13 baking dish add the stew and spread until even. Gently top with cauliflower topping, spreading it evenly and not pressing down too far. Sprinkle the remaining 1 cup of shredded cheese over the top.

Bake for 15-20 minutes until topping is puffed and cheese is browning slightly. Remove from heat and serve immediately. Sprinkle more Worcestershire Sauce on individual servings if needed.

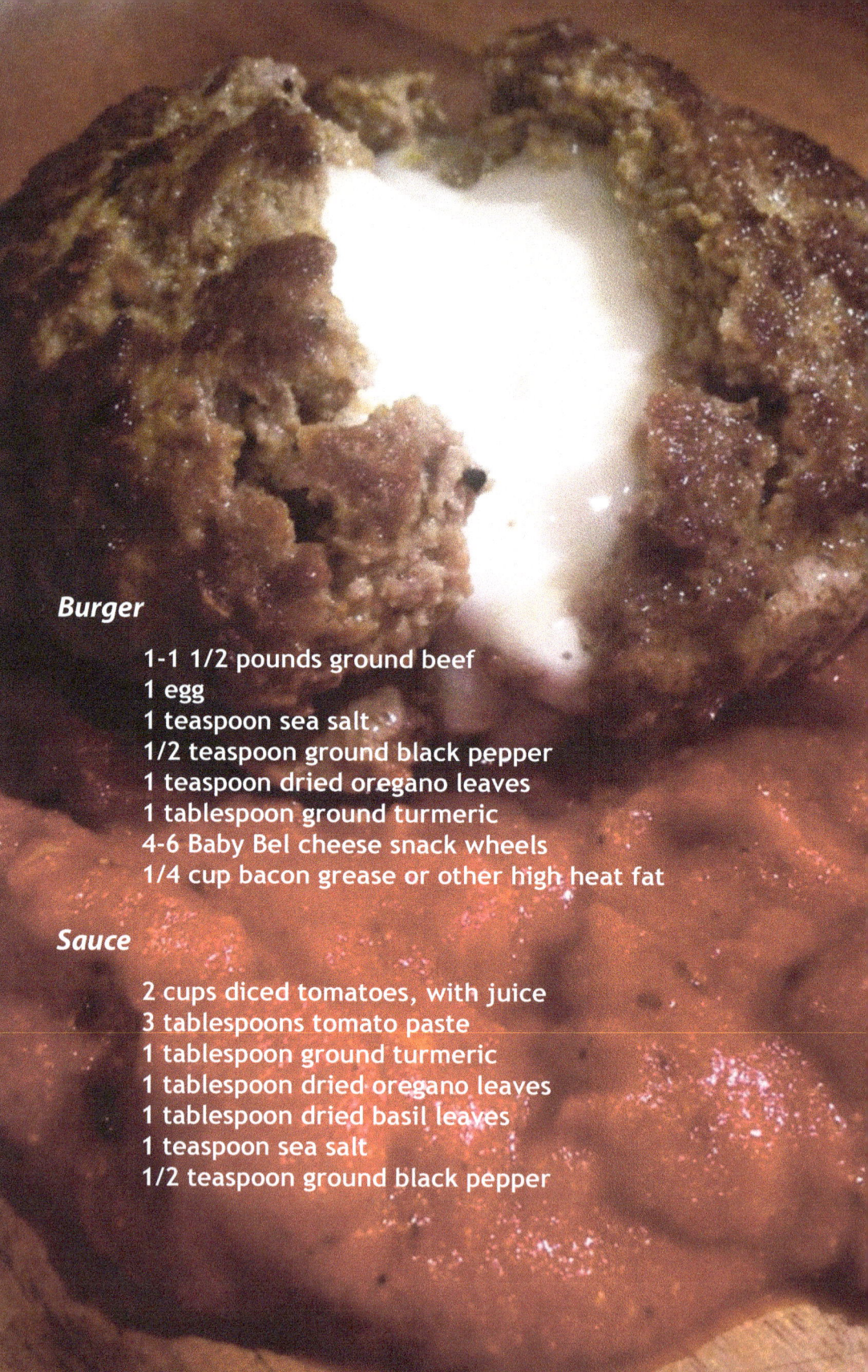

Burger

    1-1 1/2 pounds ground beef
    1 egg
    1 teaspoon sea salt
    1/2 teaspoon ground black pepper
    1 teaspoon dried oregano leaves
    1 tablespoon ground turmeric
    4-6 Baby Bel cheese snack wheels
    1/4 cup bacon grease or other high heat fat

Sauce

    2 cups diced tomatoes, with juice
    3 tablespoons tomato paste
    1 tablespoon ground turmeric
    1 tablespoon dried oregano leaves
    1 tablespoon dried basil leaves
    1 teaspoon sea salt
    1/2 teaspoon ground black pepper

Cheesy Burger Bombs

I rarely have a burger without cheese on top, so why not make some with the cheese in the middle? They were juicy and gooey and very satisfying.

First make the sauce. In medium pot combine tomatoes, tomato paste and spices (turmeric, oregano, basil, salt, and pepper). Stir and cook over medium heat until steam rises. Cover and turn heat down to simmer until burgers are ready to serve.

Remove plastic and wax wrapping from cheese wheels, then set cheese aside.

In large bowl combine the ground beef, egg and spices (salt, pepper, oregano, and turmeric). The best way to combine it all is using your hands, but because of the turmeric they may turn yellow.

Divide the beef mixture into 1/4 pound piles. Take a pile in your hand and flatten it into a patty. Place a cheese wheel in the middle of the patty and wrap the edges of the patty over the cheese. Close up the edges to completely cover the cheese. Repeat making patties until all the beef is used up.

In a frying pan heat the bacon grease over medium high heat. Place burgers in pan and cook on one side for about five minutes, until the bottoms begin to brown. Flip burgers, turn heat down to medium and cover. Cook for another 5-10 minutes, until burgers are done to your preferred doneness.

Serve immediately over a bed of the sauce spread on a serving plate.

GREEK BURGERS

These burgers are a tangy, filling meal that reminds me of my beloved gyros (pronounced 'yee-rohs' in my world). The first time I made them I had to negotiate with Little B to use the last of her Greek yogurt for tzatziki. She loves it with a little stevia, cinnamon and vanilla for dessert, but I finagled enough from her for the tzatziki.

Patties

    1/2 cup parsley, finely chopped
    2 tablespoons finely chopped fresh oregano
    1/2 cup finely chopped fresh mint
    3 cloves garlic, finely chopped
    1 teaspoon black pepper
    2 teaspoons sea salt
    1 egg
    1 tablespoon lemon juice
    2 pounds ground beef or lamb
    2 tablespoons olive oil
    1 cup feta, crumbled
    2 cups fresh spinach leaves, stems removed
    1 English cucumber, sliced in ¼" coins
    1 tomato, sliced
    1/2 red onion, thin julienne

Tzatziki

    1 cup cucumber, peeled, seeded and finely chopped
    1 1/2 cups Greek yogurt
    1 clove garlic, crushed
    2 teaspoons finely chopped fresh parsley
    2 teaspoons finely chopped fresh mint
    2-3 teaspoons lime juice
    1 tablespoon olive oil
    1/2 teaspoon sea salt
    1/4 teaspoon black pepper, finely ground

First make the tzatziki—doing it right before the meal works, but doing it the day before is better. Whisk all ingredients together. Chill until time to serve.

For patties whisk together the first eight ingredients. Pour mixture over ground meat in large bowl. Using your hands make sure the egg mixture is well combined with the meat. Form meat into patties about 4" wide and 1" deep.

In large frying pan heat the oil over medium high heat. Add patties and cook on one side until seared, about five minutes. Flip patties and sear the other side. Cover and cook to desired doneness.

On a bed of spinach and a layer of cucumber coins (either on a bun or directly on a plate) place a patty. Layer toppings—tomato slices, a glop of tzatziki, feta crumbles and onion. Dig in!

Swedish Meatballs

When I think of Swedish cuisine I imagine pastries, fish, and meatballs. My hankering to make meatballs led me to the well known Swedish meatballs. Research into the Swedish version revealed they possess a subtle, yet well-rounded flavor. The key flavors, along with the variety of ground meats, are onion, allspice and white pepper. My other meatball versions, whether cheesy or ultimate, have much less subtle flavors added. I was very curious about making the traditional Swedish dish.

Never having partaken of the meatballs on Swedish soil, I relied on my previous experiences eating them here in America. The experiences revealed they are smaller and more delicate than those huge suckers you find in an American sandwich or spaghetti.

Served on a bed of zucchini noodles and a side of acorn squash, these meatballs made for a warm, comforting winter meal. The gravy was rich and addictive, and the use of almond meal instead of breadcrumbs worked well to hold the balls together.

Balls

    3 tablespoons butter or ghee
    3 tablespoons finely grated onion
    1/3 pound ground beef*
    1/3 pound ground pork*
    1/3 pound ground veal*
    1 teaspoon allspice
    1 teaspoon sea salt
    1/4 teaspoon finely ground white pepper
    2 tablespoons almond meal
    1 egg

Gravy

Pan juices
1 cup cream or cream substitute
Sea salt to taste
Finely ground white pepper to taste

Melt 1 tablespoon of butter in an iron skillet over medium heat. Sauté onions in the butter until golden brown. Remove from heat and let cool until comfortable to handle when mixing with meats.

Place ground meats in a medium bowl. Add allspice, salt, and white pepper, almond meal, onions, and egg. Using your hands mush the ingredients until well combined. Form mix into approximately 18 meatballs, each about the size of a a golf ball. Chill meatballs for at least an hour—this will help them hold their shape when cooking.

Melt the remaining 2 tablespoons of butter in the iron skillet over medium high heat. Add the meatballs, making sure there is some space in the pan around each ball. Shake the pan as you fry the balls, to brown them evenly and prevent flat sides. Continue to cook for 10-12 minutes, until they are evenly browned on all sides.

When all of the meatballs are done cooking transfer them to a plate and place on the stove top to keep them warm.

To make the gravy, lower heat under the pan to medium. Scrape the bottom of the pan to loosen the drippings. Add the heavy cream, salt and pepper to taste. Gently stir to incorporate the cream. Simmer for about three minutes.

Pour gravy over the warm meatballs and serve immediately. Since there is no thickener in the gravy it may separate a bit if overcooked or after it sits away from the heat. If separation occurs just stir right before spooning over meatballs.

*Traditional Swedish meatballs are made with a veal, pork, and beef combination, but any combination of ground meats will work, as long as there is a total one pound.

2 pounds ground beef
1 cup sharp cheddar cheese, grated
3/4 cup black olives, chopped
2 eggs
2 cloves garlic, crushed
1 tablespoon dried parsley leaves
1 tablespoon dried basil leaves
1 teaspoon onion powder
1/2 teaspoon cumin powder
1/2 teaspoon sea salt
1/4 teaspoon black pepper, ground

Little Cheesy Meatballs

Little B was adamant about participating in choosing what to include in these balls besides meat. We decided on garlic, black olives and cheese. We tossed it all into a bowl and had a blast smooshing it all together with our hands. They were yummy, especially on top of some sautéed zucchini with some spicy sauce on top, although Little B skipped the spicy and ate them plain.

Preheat oven to 350 degrees.

Set out mini muffin pans to accommodate approximately 40 meatballs. Large shallow baking sheets will work too, but the cheese might leak out a bit.

In a large bowl add all ingredients. Using your hands, squish all the ingredients together until well combined. Mold balls to about one inch in diameter and place one in each muffin spot or place them on a baking sheet, leaving an inch around each meatball. Bake for about 20 minutes until bubbly. Remove and let cool about five minutes before plating and serving.

While the balls are baking prepare the sauce and any vegetables that will accompany the meatballs. The suggested zucchini and sauce are described below.

To make a sauce combine a small can of tomato paste and medium size can of tomatoes and chiles (or just diced tomatoes if you want milder sauce). Let simmer with a sprinkle of salt until heated through.

For the zucchini, cut up squash in two-inch pieces. Heat 1-2 tablespoons of butter, then add zucchini. Sauté with a sprinkle of salt and pepper until softened a bit, about five minutes.

Serve meatballs on top of the zucchini and top with the tomato sauce of your choosing.

Vegetable Meatloaf

This recipe stemmed from my desire to use up the vegetable odds and ends in the fridge. It worked very well, held together like meatloaf tends to not want to do.

1 1/2 pounds ground beef
2 tablespoons tomato paste
2 stalks celery
1 carrot (or 1 1/2 cups mini carrots)
1 small yellow onion
2 cups fresh spinach
4 cloves garlic
3 eggs
1/2 cup fresh parsley
1 tablespoon dried thyme leaves
1 teaspoon ground cumin
1 teaspoon sea salt
1/2 teaspoon ground black pepper
1 teaspoon paprika
1 cup sharp cheddar cheese, grated

Preheat oven to 350 degrees.

In a food processor add tomato paste, celery, carrot, onion, spinach, garlic, eggs, thyme, cumin, salt, pepper, and paprika. Pulse until vegetables are very small pieces and herbs are combined. In large bowl combine beef and vegetable mixture.

With your bare hands mix meat and vegetables until all the meat is coated and the vegetables are combined with the meat. Press mixture into rectangular bread pan.

Bake for 45-55 minutes, until cooked through.

Sprinkle top of loaf with cheese and place in hot oven with heat off for five to ten minutes, until cheese is melted. Remove from oven and let rest for about five minutes.

Slice in pan, arrange on serving tray, and serve.

1 1/2 pounds ground beef
2 large eggs
2 cups crumbled feta cheese
1 cup chopped raw spinach
1 cup chopped kalamata olives
1 cup chopped marinated artichoke hearts
1 cup finely chopped onion
4 cloves garlic, crushed
1/4 cup chopped fresh mint
1/4 cup fresh oregano leaves
1/2 cup chopped fresh parsley
1 tablespoon sea salt
1 teaspoon ground black pepper
8-10 slices bacon, uncooked

Mediterranean Meatloaf

I have shared a couple of different meatloaf recipes already, like the spicy one and the veggie one, but never one wrapped in bacon, until now! This one has a bit of a Greek twist. I would blame other things, but the extreme moistness of this loaf I attribute to the bacon.

As with many baked meals, it tastes great the day it is made, but after sitting in the fridge and reheating, it is even better!

Preheat oven to 350 degrees.

In a large bowl place the ground beef. Add the eggs, cheese, spinach, olives, artichoke hearts, onion, garlic, herbs, salt, and pepper. Using your hands, break up egg yolks and squish other bowl contents together with meat until well combined.

Press meat mixture evenly into 9×9 inch baking dish or large loaf pan.

Arrange bacon slices on top of the meat in a criss cross pattern, tucking the ends around the sides of the meat. Gently press down on the loaf to avoid any uneven shaping resulting from tucking the bacon.

Bake in oven for one hour. Remove and let sit for about ten minutes before removing to serving dish, then serve.

Pork

Cornless Tamales

If you have ever eaten tamales, you know there is a specific texture to the masa portion, and there is supposed to be a hint of smoky spiciness to the middle meat filling. Some people may be on the verge of offended when I talk about masa without corn, for the word typically represents a corn-based dough used for all kinds of dishes, including pupusas, tortillas and of course tamales.

For our version we used flaxseed meal and coconut flour to achieve the required texture. We also used what may seem like a lot of salt, but with the flaxseed and coconut products it is needed, to give a little help to the pork for it all to work together and carry the spice flavors through to the final dish.

These tamales turn out flavorful and robust, able to compete (in a good way) with the toppings we traditionally serve with them, and with a texture almost exactly like corn-based masa.

Masa

- 2 cups coconut flour
- 2 cups golden flaxseed meal
- 1/4 pound lard, melted
- 2 eggs
- 2 tablespoons ground cumin
- 1 tablespoon garlic powder
- 1 tablespoon chili powder
- 3 tablespoons sea salt
- 5-6 cups liquid retained from meat filling
- 24-36 corn husks*, soaked in water for at least one hour

Filling

- 2 pound pork roast
- 2 tablespoons lard or bacon grease
- 1 small onion, diced
- 5 cloves garlic, crushed
- 1 tablespoon cumin seeds
- 2 jalapeños, diced
- 1 cup roasted green chiles (canned or fresh), diced

    2 chipotle peppers with adobo sauce from can (use about 1 tablespoon of sauce)
    1 cup water
    2 tablespoons sea salt

Toppings

    1 Batch beef chili
    1 Batch Guacamole
    1 Batch Chimichurri
    1 Batch Queso (1 pound Velveeta melted with 1 can Rotel tomatoes and chiles)
    Sour Cream

Sear sides of the pork roast in a large skillet, then place roast in a crock pot.

In the same skillet add bacon grease and melt over medium-high heat. When melted add onion, garlic, cumin seeds, jalapeño, and chiles. Cook until seared. Add chipotle peppers and adobo sauce to mixture and continue cooking until combined and heated through.

Transfer seared mixture to crock pot over the roast. Add salt and water, then cook roast on low for 8-10 hours. Turn crock pot off and let cool for a few hours. Drain liquid and shred meat with a fork, retaining the liquid for masa.

In a mixer bowl combine flaxseed meal, coconut flour, cumin, salt, and garlic powder. Add lard and eggs to mixture and combine into a dough. Add liquid from the meat one cup at a time until it is the consistency of soft peanut butter—you will need anywhere from four to six cups of liquid.

To build the tamales pat dry one corn husk, then lay it flat on your work surface. Spread masa evenly in the middle of the husk, leaving 1-2 inches clear at the top and bottom, and along one side. Drop a row of pork along the middle of the masa, to the very edges of where it is spread.

Gently roll the tamale, making sure the masa completely envelopes the pork in the middle. Overlap the sides of the husk and fold the small end up. A small strip of husk can be used to tie around the tamale to keep it closed, or just lay completed tamales face down on seam side to avoid unrolling. Repeat process until you run out of supplies.

In a deep stock pot with pasta/steamer insert, fill bottom

of pot with water, but no higher than the bottom of the steamer insert—tamales should not be sitting in water at all.

Fill the insert with tamales by lining them up vertically, with folded end down. Place cover on pot and heat to boiling, then turn heat down to simmer, making sure steam continues to rise. Steam tamales for about one hour, until the masa is firm and they are heated through.

Remove tamales from pan and lay out in a single layer, allowing them to dry out a bit. When ready to eat, unroll the tamales from the husk and eat plain or smother with your toppings of choice.

Note: If you prefer not to use corn husks, parchment paper does very well as a substitute!

Stuffed Poblano Peppers

Did you ever go to a Mexican restaurant, order a chile relleno and end up with a kinda tasteless mound, filled mostly with rice and covered with soggy, sometimes slightly under cooked batter? Here is a way to avoid all that unpleasantness! A little more effort is needed to fill out the other elements of your own traditional combination platter, but here is some help with enchiladas, salsa, and guacamole.

Since I do not dip these peppers in batter I chose not to char and remove the skins. With all the cooking and liquid the peppers cook up soft and skin is not tough. This is a a great recipe for using leftover meat and vegetables. It also works great with other large pepper types.

- 4 Poblano peppers
- 4 ounces cream cheese, room temperature
- 2 cups cooked shredded pork or cooked seasoned ground beef
- 1 cup cooked and chopped green cabbage
- 1 cup canned diced tomatoes
- 1 teaspoon dried oregano
- 1 teaspoon ground cumin
- 1 clove garlic
- Sea salt and pepper to taste
- 2 cups shredded cheddar and Monterrey Jack cheese
- 1/2 cup water
- Sour cream and lime wedges for serving

Preheat oven to 400 degrees.

Make one slit in each pepper lengthwise. Remove seeds and membrane from inside, careful to leave the stem attached to the pepper. Sprinkle inside of each pepper with salt.

In blender or food processor combine tomatoes, oregano, cumin, and a dash each of salt and pepper. Purée until you have a smooth tomato sauce. Set aside.

Divide cream cheese into four pieces. With the back of your spoon (or your fingers if you don't mind a little mess) spread the cream cheese around in the cavity of the pepper.

In a medium bowl combine the meat and cabbage. Stuff the meat and cabbage mixture in the pepper, making sure the slit does not tear open any more than necessary.

Top the meat and cabbage with the tomato sauce, making sure it drizzles down into the pepper. Top with the shredded cheese, tucking it in under the edges of the peppers, then gently pushing the pepper edges together as far as you can.

In a baking dish just big enough to hold the peppers snugly (9x9 or 8x11) pour in the water, then add the peppers. Cover loosely with foil and bake for 20 minutes.

Remove foil and bake for 20-30 more minutes, until cheese begins to brown. Remove from oven and let cool for about five minutes before serving.

Serve with a dollop of sour cream and a lime wedge for drizzling.

Creamy Coated Pork Chops

I go to the store once a week, with the hope that additional trips will be unnecessary. I do pretty well on that score most weeks. I also go with a pretty flexible list. I know there will be replacement of standard condiments we have run out of, as well staples like fruits, vegetables, protein and cheese. Beyond that I rely on prices for the most part.

Is chicken or pork on sale? Is the deli sliced ham or beef cheaper this week? Is the cabbage or cauliflower cheaper? You get the idea. Sometimes I do have specific dishes in mind, but usually it is a matter of having a stocked fridge and freezer. This time the pork chops won the price battle, so here is the lovely result of living not so large at the store!

- 4-6 thin pork chops, with or without bone
- 1 cup mayonnaise
- 2 tablespoons horseradish mustard (or 1 tablespoon yellow mustard and 1 tablespoon prepared horseradish)
- 1 teaspoon sea salt
- 2 tablespoons garlic powder
- 3 tablespoons dehydrated onion
- 3 tablespoons lemon juice
- Sea salt and pepper to taste

Preheat oven to 400 degrees.

In medium bowl combine the mayonnaise, mustard, garlic, salt, onion and lemon juice. Whisk together until blended.

Generously season chops with salt and pepper. Arrange chops on shallow baking sheet. Spread mayonnaise mixture over the top of all the chops.

Bake on the middle rack of the oven for 30 to 40 minutes, until top of chops has browned and internal temperature measures at least 145 degrees. Serve immediately.

Stuffed Portobello Mushrooms

I have mentioned in the past my long relationship with portobello mushrooms, their meatiness without being meat, and how well they work as a base for pizza and all things baked. This recipe is easy to put together and slide in the oven.

- 4 large portobello mushrooms
- 3/4 cup ranch dressing
- 1/2 pound ground hot Italian pork sausage
- 3/4 cup chopped white onion
- 8 slices cheese
- 1 batch guacamole (optional)
- Sea salt and ground black pepper to taste

Gently cook sausage in a frying pan over medium heat, breaking it up into bite-sized pieces, but not too small. It can be left slightly pink, for it will finish cooking with the mushrooms.

Preheat oven to 350 degrees.

Place mushrooms cap side down on work surface, leaving the stems attached but trimming the end of the stems. Season with sea salt and pepper. With the back of a spoon spread ranch dressing* on the gills of the mushrooms. Place sausage pieces on the gills, surrounding the stem. Sprinkle onion on top of the sausage.

Place two pieces of cheese on top of each mushroom, making sure most of the sausage and onion are covered.

Place mushrooms on baking sheet. Place sheet in oven and bake for 45 minutes to one hour. The cheese should be melted and starting to brown.

Remove from oven and let cool for five minutes. Serve plain or with guacamole.

Seafood

Salmon Stuffed Mushrooms

For this dish I didn't want to overwhelm the salmon with other flavors, so I stuck with ingredients I often use when poaching the salmon. Being surrounded by mushroom, cream cheese, and egg whites, the salmon did not get dried out or overcooked.

15-20 miniature Portobello mushrooms
3 garlic cloves, minced
1 tablespoon extra virgin olive oil
2 egg whites
6 ounces poached salmon
1/2 + 1/4 teaspoon fresh dill
1/2 cup cream cheese, softened
1/2 cup water
Salt and pepper to taste

Scoop out stem and meat from caps of mushrooms. Chop the stems finely.

In a small skillet over medium heat add the oil. When oil is hot add the mushroom stems and garlic. Stir occasionally until mushrooms have released moisture and liquid is reduced, about five minutes. Remove from heat.

In medium bowl whisk egg white until foamy but not stiff, about 15 seconds. Add to the whites the cream cheese, salmon, 1/2 teaspoon dill and stir until combined. Add the stem mixture. Add salt and pepper to taste.

Preheat oven to 350 degrees.

Fill mushroom caps with cheese mixture. Place filled caps evenly distributed in a 9×13 baking dish.

In a measuring cup mix the water with 1/4 teaspoon salt and 1/4 teaspoon dill. Stir until salt is dissolved. Pour water into bottom of baking dish.

Bake in oven for 30 minutes, until mushroom caps shrink and filling puffs up. Remove from oven. Place mushrooms onto platter and serve immediately.

SALMON PATTIES

I got nostalgic on this one, in many respects. I was craving salmon and began remembering the patties my mom used to make with the canned stuff when I was little. I liked them, but always got a little shiver when I came across one of the soft, yet still crunchy pieces of bone from the canned salmon. I still recall not being able to decide whether the shiver was fun or not. The soft bone was easily chewable but always a surprise in the otherwise non-crunchy dish. Another nostalgia point was from my time living in Juneau, Alaska. In late summer and early fall the salmon pile up on each other in an effort to swim upstream and practically jump out of the water into your arms. You have to make sure they are not aiming for bear arms, but after the all clear on the bear front, you can just grab the slippery suckers.

Living in Juneau you are surrounded by fisherpeople who get their maximum catch as often as they can and they share share share. It can be smoked, steamed, grilled, marinated, chopped, dried, jarred, canned...which brings me to this recipe. For this recipe I used canned pink salmon, which can be found that was wild caught from Alaska. Not ideal, but effective in my effort to combine the nostalgia, and the fact that the only fresh salmon found in Maryland is Atlantic. Sigh. And as Big D said, these were the first salmon patties he ever had that were not dry and Little B enjoyed them, too. Score!

- 1 can pink salmon, drained with spine and other bones removed
- 1/3 cup plain Greek yogurt
- 3 eggs
- 1 lemon, juiced with meat included
- 1/2-2/3 cup golden flaxseed meal
- 1/2 teaspoon sea salt
- 1/2 teaspoon dried dill
- 1 teaspoon dried thyme leaves
- 1 teaspoon dried parsley leaves
- 1 clove garlic, crushed
- 1/2 cup coconut oil

In medium bowl add salmon and break it up into small flakes.

Make a pool in the middle of the salmon and drop in yogurt, eggs, salt, thyme, parsley, garlic and dill. Whisk together egg, lemon juice and yogurt mixture with a fork until eggs are broken up. Toss egg mixture with salmon on the edges of the bowl until combined. Add 1/2 cup of the flaxseed meal and stir. Let sit for a minute or two, allowing the flaxseed to expand.

While you wait add the coconut oil to a medium skillet and heat to medium high. If the salmon mixture is not thick enough to drop into the oil and hold shape as patties (thicker than pancake batter, thinner than, say, tuna salad) add some more meal and stir it in until thicker.

Drop a large spoonful of mixture into the skillet and gently flatten so it is of even thickness and about two inches in diameter. Cook until the patties set and begin to brown on the edges, about 2 minutes. Gently flip the patties and cook for another minute or two.

Repeat process until all the patties are cooked. Since the only raw ingredient is the egg, the patties only need to be cooked just long enough brown a bit and to cook the egg in the mixture.

Serve immediately with a side of veggies.

Creamy Shrimp Alfredo

If you had not noticed from my Shrimp with Lemon Cream Sauce I make, I really like creamy sauces. I love Alfredo sauce, although not necessarily on fettuccine anymore, and my favorite pasta dish of all time is spaghetti carbonara. Since I was craving the carbonara and Big D was craving the Alfredo, and we were being stared down by the spaghetti squash and shrimp in the fridge, I combined all the pieces into a quiet, Saturday night dinner.

Depending on the history you believe, the original Alfredo sauce did not actually have any cream, and the original carbonara sauce did not have it either, but I think it all came together in a rich, satisfying dish. I even added a nod to the carbonara's pancetta with the bacon grease used for the squash and shrimp. Other fats like butter or olive oil or coconut oil could be used, too, but when there is bacon grease available, why? It turned out great and made me want to watch The Godfather or The Untouchables.

- 1 1/2 cups heavy cream
- 1/2 cup butter
- 2 egg yolks
- 1 clove garlic, crushed
- 1 cup freshly grated Parmesan cheese plus extra for serving
- 3 tablespoons bacon grease
- 3 cloves garlic, finely chopped
- 3 tablespoons fresh parsley, finely chopped
- 2 pounds large shrimp, shelled and deveined
- 1 large spaghetti squash
- Salt to taste

Preheat oven to 350 degrees.

Slice squash lengthwise and scrape out seeds and stringy membrane. Place squash halves face down and place in the oven. Bake for 45 minutes to an hour, until center is soft and edges begin to brown. Remove from oven and let cool enough to handle.

While the squash bakes prepare the sauce. In a cold medium sauce pan add the cream and egg yolk. Whisk together until well combined. Add 1/2 cup butter and turn on heat to medium, stirring occasionally. When the butter is melted and sauce begins to steam, but not boil, add the garlic. Continue to stir and avoid boiling.

Begin to add the cheese, stirring constantly, about 1/4 cup at a time, making sure it is completely melted before adding more. When all the cheese is incorporated add some salt to taste, if needed. Turn heat down to low simmer and let sauce simmer and thicken, but not boil!!!

With a fork scrape out the cooled squash 'spaghetti' and place in a bowl. Toss with a sprinkling of salt and 1 tablespoon bacon grease or other fat. Set aside until time to serve.

In a large skillet melt 2 tablespoons bacon grease over medium heat. Add garlic and stir until garlic begins to sweat. Increase heat under burner to medium high. Add shrimp, sprinkle lightly with salt, and toss regularly until shrimp begins to turn pink. Sprinkle with parsley and continue tossing until shrimp is cooked through, about three to five minutes.

To serve, place a bed of spaghetti squash on a plate, top with shrimp and drizzle with sauce. Serve immediately with Parmesan cheese on the side.

Shrimp with Lemon Cream Sauce

There is a story/urban legend known down in Texas about a restaurant called Paesano's. It was (and still is) popular for a Texas version of Italian, including a particular shrimp dish. The shrimp is butterflied and gently dragged through flour and lightly cooked in softly boiling oil. A creamy lemon sauce is made and poured over the top. Totally addictive. I don't know how true the story is, but here is what I heard many years ago. The married couple who owned the restaurant got divorced. Rumor has it the husband got the restaurant, but the wife got the recipes. It was not enough to have the recipes, so to even the score she widely distributed them and they gradually crept into kitchens far and wide. Eventually I got a fuzzy copy of the recipe titled 'shrimp Paesano.' I used to make it all the time, laden with flour and served on top of linguine or angel hair pasta. Each time I made it the kitchen is left fragrant and an absolute mess—multiple pots and pans dirty, the counter sprinkled with shrimp shells and flour, but some beautifully presented shrimp resting on a pile of creamy, lemony pasta with sauce. I think I usually remember the mess in the kitchen because you serve immediately and don't do the final clean up until much later, after food coma passes.

For this recipe you need to drop everything right when the shrimp is ready and sit down and eat. Of course, the dishes are always waiting when dinner is through, just a little stickier than I prefer. Here is my attempt to make a version more in line with our less expensive, grain free, low carb eating habits. The kitchen still is a mess when all is said and done, but the flavor shines through just like the original.

- 1 pound large shrimp or langostinos, shelled
- 2 eggs, whisked
- 3/4 cup plus 2 tablespoons butter
- 3 lemons, juiced with meat and seeds removed (about ¾ cup)

4 cloves garlic, crushed
2 cups heavy cream
1/2 cup grated Parmesan cheese
1 teaspoon arrowroot powder
    (optional—final sauce will be thinner without)
1 medium or large spaghetti squash
1 cup extra virgin olive oil
Sea salt to taste
Fresh parsley springs (optional for serving)

    Preheat oven to 400 degrees.
    Cut spaghetti squash in half and scrape out seeds. Place halves face down on baking sheet. Place in oven and bake for about 45 minutes, until meat is soft. Scrape out meat with a fork to make spaghetti 'noodles.' Melt 2 tablespoons butter into noodles and sprinkle lightly with salt. Cover and keep warm until time to serve.
    While the squash cooks prepare the sauce and prep the shrimp or langostinos. In a large skillet over medium heat melt 2 tablespoons butter. Add shellfish and gently toss, only cooking long enough so they shellfish is only half cooked—the rest of the cooking will happen later when simmering in the sauce. Set aside the shellfish and make the sauce.
    In medium sauce pan over medium heat melt 3/4 cup butter. Add all the lemon juice and garlic. Heat until steamy. Add cream, lower heat and cook until sauce is mixed well, stirring frequently. Add cheese and stir slowly, making sure it melts and blends in with the smooth sauce. Add arrowroot powder (optional) and whisk. Sauce should bubble slightly and thicken, but not fully boil.
    Add shellfish and gently simmer for about five more minutes, allowing the shellfish to cook through completely. Remove from heat and keep covered.
    On individual serving plates make a bed of spaghetti squash, then on top generously place a ladle full of shellfish and sauce. Add parsley if you like and serve immediately.

BREADS & CRUSTS

GRAIN FREE PIZZA CRUST

We don't get pizza delivered around here—nobody I know of delivers grain free pizza—so we have to do our own thing.

The pizza we make is always loaded with a lot of garlic and a whole pile of toppings. The important part is the awesome crust. It holds the toppings without getting soggy, and there is no doughy crust getting in the way of the garlic.

Did I mention we use a lot of garlic? Oh, and we use a bunch of garlic, which is not mandatory, but we like a lot of garlic on our pizza. Garlic in the crust, garlic cooked with the mushrooms, and garlic sprinkled between the layers of topping. And a last sprinkle of garlic on the top layer of cheese.

Any topping combination you like will work on top of the crust, especially garlic.

Crust

- 2 cups shredded mozzarella cheese
- 2 tablespoons coconut flour
- 2 tablespoons golden flaxseed meal
- 1/4 teaspoon baking soda
- 2 teaspoons dried parsley
- 1 teaspoon dried basil
- 1 teaspoon garlic powder
- 1/2 teaspoon onion powder
- 1/2 teaspoon sea salt
- 2 large eggs, beaten

Suggested Toppings:

- 1/2 cup ranch dressing or pizza sauce
- 1 tablespoon extra virgin olive oil
- 1/2 pound ground Italian sausage
- 1 cup thin sliced pepperoni
- 1 cup sliced mushrooms
- 4 cloves garlic, sliced
- 1/2 cup chopped black olives
- 2 cups shredded mozzarella cheese

1 cup shredded sharp cheddar cheese
1/2 cup grated Parmesan cheese

Before making the crust make sure all the toppings you plan to use are prepared.

If you are using the suggested toppings first cook the sausage/mushroom/garlic topping. In a medium sauté pan over medium heat add the olive oil. When the oil is hot add the garlic and cook until it softens. Add the sausage, breaking it up into bite sized pieces. When the sausage is half cooked add the mushrooms and toss the whole mess around until the sausage is done and the mushrooms are at least heated through.

Preheat oven to 425F, then prepare the crust.

In a medium bowl combine the dry ingredients with the cheese. Add the eggs and stir until combined. It will be a bit sticky and not look at all like pizza dough. That is okay.

If you are making the pizza on a cookie sheet here are the directions. Cover a large cookie sheet with parchment paper. Spread the dough on the paper, making a very thin layer. The best way to spread it is to press down on it with your fingers-it helps to have a little bit of oil on your fingers to reduce the stickiness. It won't spread out to all the edges, but it will cover most of the pan. The layer should be no more than 1/8 inch thick. Place pan in oven and cook just until it puffs up and the edges and top begin to brown, about seven minutes.

If you are using an enameled pizza stone preheat it. Spread enough dough onto the pizza stone or baking dish to have a layer about 1/4 inch deep. On a preheated pizza stone the dough begins to soften as soon as it touches the surface so make sure you commit when dropping it onto the stone. Bake the crust for no more than five minutes, allowing it to set and just begin to brown.

Reduce the oven temperature to 400F.

Remove the crust from the oven and begin piling on the toppings. We usually start with a thin layer of ranch dressing or your favorite pizza sauce, followed by some cheddar cheese, sausage/mushroom/garlic, mozzarella cheese, then pepperoni and olives, followed by a mix of cheddar, mozzarella and last but not least Parmesan.

If you like your pizza herby, then do what we do and sprinkle some parsley, basil and garlic between the layers of toppings. Bake the pizza for 15-20 minutes, until the cheese in the middle is melted and edges are starting to turn brown.

Remove from the oven and let cool for at least five minutes before cutting.

Almond Pizza Crust

A long time ago Big D and I started a tradition of pizzabeer. No, that is not a typo. We would go to a spot—whether it was in Alaska, Virginia, Nevada, Texas...wherever we were, we would sit and eat pizza, drink beer and have long, winding talks about where we were going together. Sometimes they were about short term goals, other times they were longer term. Regardless, they were talks over food and beverage. Without some effort it is difficult now to go out to a restaurant and have grain free pizzabeer.

When making pizza these days we do it at home and we regularly use a grain free crust figured out a couple of years ago. It is delicious, but includes flaxseed meal and coconut flour, which gives it a nuttier taste than what we like for some pizzas.

This version of a grain free crust is made by relying on almond meal and cheese. It makes for a crust that can hold the excess of toppings we are wont to use, while not adding a ton of strong flavor.

Just think about it—when you eat pizza are you tasting the crust, or is it the toppings? I realized when I was pondering pizza that what I missed most from the wheaty/grainy versions was the toppings, not the crust taste, and the ability to pick up a piece of pizza and take a big bite.

We stumbled upon this more subtle tasting version one night when we wanted pizza and were woefully short of coconut flour and flaxseed meal needed for our grain free pizza crust. It puffs more on the edges than out other version, and gave us the more neutral flavor we were looking for. Necessity is the mother of invention, right?

Crust

- 4 cups shredded mozzarella cheese
- 6 tablespoons almond flour
- 1 teaspoon baking soda
- 2 teaspoons dried parsley flakes
- 1 teaspoon dried basil
- 1 teaspoon garlic powder
- 1/2 teaspoon onion powder

1 teaspoon sea salt
2 eggs, beaten

Suggested Toppings

1/2 cup pizza sauce or tomato paste
1 cup mozzarella cheese and cheddar cheese, grated and mixed
20-24 pepperoni slices
1/2 cup black olives, chopped
Sprinkling of finely chopped basil and oregano

Preheat oven to 450 degrees.

If using an enameled pizza stone prepare as directed. A pizza stone without enamel may be too porous to use this crust recipe, but it has not been tested.

If you are making the pizza on a cookie sheet, cover a large cookie sheet with parchment paper. Spread the dough on the paper, making a very thin layer. The best way to spread it is to press down on it with your fingers-it helps to have a little bit of oil on your fingers to reduce the stickiness. It won't spread out to all the edges, but it will cover most of the pan. The layer should be no more than 1/8 inch thick. Place pan in oven and cook just until it puffs up and the edges and top begin to brown, about seven minutes.

Combine together in a medium bowl all ingredients except the eggs. When well combined add the eggs and stir with a fork until a moist dough forms.

Spread enough dough onto the pizza stone or baking dish to have a layer about 1/4 inch deep. On a preheated pizza stone the dough begins to soften as soon as it touches the surface so make sure you commit when dropping it onto the stone.

Bake the crust for no more than five minutes, allowing it to set and just begin to brown.

Lower oven temperature to 425 degrees. Remove crust from oven and add sauce, toppings and cheese. Return to oven and bake for 10-15 minutes, until top is browning at the highest points.

Let cool for about ten minutes, allowing crust to set and toppings to cool. Slice and serve.

BRED BREAD

As our grain free journey evolved we longed more and more for sandwiches and other bready foods. We thought there must be a way to make a nutritious, grain free bread-like thing to sate our desires. Some grain free breads out there on the market are okay, but are more rubbery and tasteless than we like. After experimenting with various baked goods, we were already familiar with the impact of flaxseed meals, coconut flour, and almond meal—in muffins, pies, rolls, etc. Not only their impact on the end product, but on our personal weight management, which was positive.

This bread is substantial enough for deli sandwiches, garlic bread, and especially grilled cheese sandwiches. After mastering the basic Bred recipe we found that some slight variations make for different, yet still satisfying results.

The 'rye' version has the tang of traditional rye bread, making for wonderful Reuben sandwiches. The version using brown flaxseed meal gives the bread a much lighter, almost poppy seed flavor that lends itself to more delicate tea and fish sandwiches.

If you miss the very obvious point here, we are so very excited to have bread back in our diet! It adds variety and convenience and helps in stretching out leftovers, which are always hanging out in our fridge.

4 cups almond flour
1/4 cup coconut flour
1/2 cup golden flaxseed meal
1 1/2 teaspoons sea salt
2 teaspoons baking soda
10 eggs
2 tablespoons melted lard, butter or coconut oil
1/4 cup apple cider vinegar

"Rye" Version

When combining first six ingredients also add:

1 tablespoon caraway seeds
1 teaspoon ground turmeric

1/2 teaspoon ground mustard
1/4 teaspoon ground black pepper

Lighter Version

Use brown flaxseed meal instead of golden

Preheat oven to 325 degrees.

Place almond four, coconut flour, flaxseed meal, salt, and baking soda in a bowl and stir until well mixed. If you are making a rye version add the rye ingredients.

In a separate bowl add eggs and lard and stir until well combined. Add vinegar and stir until well combined.

Add mixture of dry ingredients and mix on medium high speed until the wet ingredients are fully incorporated.

Grease an 9"x5" bread pan. Place dough in the pan, with fingers dampened by water, press dough into the corners of the pan, and finish by leveling out the top evenly.

Bake for 50-55 minutes, until top is brown.

If the edges of the bread have not already pulled away from the edges, gently run a narrow knife along the sides. Immediately flip the loaf onto a cooling rack and let finish cooling.

If not eating immediately the bread should be stored in the refrigerator or freezer.

1 cup coconut flour
1/4 cup golden flaxseed meal
1/2 teaspoon sea salt
1 teaspoon baking soda
9 eggs, room temperature
1/4 cup apple cider vinegar
1 cup melted lard, butter or extra virgin olive oil*

POWER (PALEO) BREAD

This. This is it! We call it power bread because of how much protein and fiber you get from a slice or two. Little B has a slice with peanut butter and forgets about food for hours. This is significant because she is often an eating machine. The bread works like a sponge, filling up your stomach quickly after eating.

The loaf and bun versions are very popular with the customers of Grain Free Haven. Customers stock up each week at farmers' markets and via our free deliveries.

I hope you make and enjoy our masterpiece! Be careful though, because one slice will fill you and a second may stuff you!

Preheat oven to 325 degrees.

In a medium bowl combine coconut flour, golden flaxseed meal, salt, and baking soda, then stir until well blended.

In a mixing bowl combine eggs and apple cider vinegar. Whisk together until egg whites and yolks are well combined. Add lard/butter/oil to eggs and continue whisking. Add the dry ingredients and continue mixing until fully incorporated.

For one loaf: pour dough into well greased 8"x4" loaf pan. Wet your hands and even out the top of the loaf, making sure it is level and damp. Bake a single loaf, on the center shelf (third shelf from the top) for 50-55 minutes.

For 6 buns: well grease six 1-cup ramekins. Place a round of parchment paper on the bottom of each, making sure the paper does not run up the sides. Using a large ice cream scoop place two level scoops into each ramekin. Wet your hands even out the top of each bun, making sure each is level and damp. Place all six ramekins on a shallow baking dish as far apart from each other as possible. Bake buns on the center shelf (third shelf from the top) for 28-32 minutes.

*Coconut oil can also be used to make this bread, but it significantly emphasizes the coconut flavor of the coconut flour. Not using coconut oil give the bread a more neutral flavor.

**This is a smaller loaf pan than typically used with wheat-based breads. The size allows for a square loaf. A larger pan can be used, but you will have more of a rectangular end result.

4 cups almond flour
4 tablespoons coconut flour
1/2 cup golden flaxseed meal
1 1/2 teaspoon sea salt
8 eggs
2 tablespoons coconut oil or lard
4 tablespoons apple cider vinegar
Butter (or other fat) for cooking plates

Robust Tortillas

I cannot believe how freakingly awesome these tortillas are! Freakingly! Not a speck of wheat or corn, but the taste and texture reminds me of some delicious, substantial homemade corn tortillas made at a little south Texas restaurant I love to frequent.

As with a few other recipes, we discovered that some quick cooking in a microwave made for some satisfying low carb substitutes for otherwise carby buns and desserts.

We spent many an evening experimenting with different thicknesses and cooking times. They can be smaller and thicker, like a gordita tortilla, thin like a corn tortilla or big and thick like a wheat flour tortilla. They have returned to our menu things like breakfast tacos, tostadas and the ever popular fajita tacos.

Now, the recipe says to spread a thin layer of batter on a plate with wet hands. I really mean a thin layer, like you can see the plate through it. For thicker ones you just need to see less of the plate.

One last note—these guys keep well in the fridge, so make a big batch and eat them all week.

Place almond four, coconut flour, flaxseed meal, salt, and baking soda in a bowl and stir until well mixed.

Add eggs, vinegar, and oil and stir until well combined, using your hands if necessary—it should be thin batter. Spread a thin layer of butter in the middle of a dinner plate. Drop about 3 level tablespoons of batter on the plate. Using wet hands spread batter from the middle to the outer edge until it is the desired size and very thin.

Have nearby a flat bottomed bowl or plate nearby to press down on the tortilla when it comes out of the oven.

Microwave for approximately 2 minutes, until the middle is cooked evenly. Immediately press down firmly for a few seconds with the bowl or plate on top of the warm tortilla. Slide off of the plate and let cool. Repeat process until all the batter is used up. Serve or refrigerate in an airtight container.

Quick Muffins

These muffins are quick, easy, and I give two different flour/meal choices, but I share them together in spite of the very different results.

Flaxseed gives a more 'grainy' texture, which goes well with burgers or for sandwiches.

The almond meal is smooth and spongier for desserts or to slather with jam. Pick what pleases you.

>   1-2 tablespoons butter or oil
>   1/2 to 1/3 cup golden flaxseed meal or almond meal
>   1 teaspoon baking powder
>   Dash pure stevia powder
>   (equivalent to 1 teaspoon pure cane sugar)
>   1 large egg

In large microwaveable mug—about 16 ounce capacity—melt butter (less butter makes for a dryer muffin).

Add dry ingredients and stir. If you want a shorter, denser muffin use the lower quantity of meal.

Add egg and mix until fully incorporated.

Place mug in microwave. Cook on high one minute. The use of almond meal often needs an additional 30 seconds if the middle is still sunken after one minute.

When cooked through remove from microwave and immediately flip muffin out of mug. Serve.

Cinnamon Rolls

Between Big D's love for cinnamon rolls and my extensive time spent in airports sniffling the wafting aromas from the cinnamon roll denizens who live there, these treats are cherished and often longed for. I am ecstatic about finally making some and feeling indulgent without grains.

Pastry

>3 medium eggs
>1/2 cup butter or coconut oil, softened
>1 teaspoon pure stevia powder
>>(equivalent to 3/4 cup pure cane sugar)
>
>1/2 cup coconut flour
>1/2 cup blanched almond flour
>1/2 teaspoon aluminum free baking powder
>1/2 teaspoon Celtic sea salt
>1 teaspoon vanilla extract

Filling

>3 tablespoons coconut oil or Butter, softened
>2 tablespoons ground cinnamon
>1 teaspoon pure stevia powder
>>(equivalent to 3/4 cup pure cane sugar)

Frosting

>6 tablespoons cream cheese, softened
>3 tablespoons butter, softened
>1/4 teaspoon pure stevia powder
>>(equivalent to 1/4 cup pure cane sugar)
>
>A little heavy cream (to thin it out, if desired)

Pastry: Whisk the eggs well. Add vanilla and stevia, then continue whisking until thoroughly combined. In a medium bowl, cream the butter until very smooth. Add in the egg/stevia combination and mix well. In another bowl mix together the coconut flour, almond four, salt, and baking powder. Slowly add the dry ingredients into the wet. Stir until a thick dough forms. Cover and place in fridge to chill the dough for 1 hour or overnight.

Frosting: Place all ingredients into a medium sized bowl and combine until smooth. Store in fridge overnight. When you start the Pastry Again section below remove Frosting from the fridge.

Filling: Mix all ingredients together.

Pastry Again: Place a sheet of parchment on counter, then spray with coconut oil spray. Place dough on greased parchment, push the dough down a bit, and spray with another layer of coconut oil. Top with another sheet of parchment. Roll the dough out with a rolling pin until a long rectangle shape, about one foot long. Remove the top layer of parchment.

Spread filling evenly over the dough. Roll up dough, with the longer side becoming the roll, using the edge of the parchment to make a tight log. Cut into 1 1/2 inch pieces.

Place the rolls into a greased muffin tin or onto a cookie sheet about 1 inch apart. Bake in a preheated 350 degree oven for 15-20 minutes or until baked through. Insert a toothpick to check doneness...the toothpick should come out clean.

Spread the frosting on the rolls. Serve immediately to family members who were drooling over the smell of the baking rolls. Store extras in airtight container for up to one week at room temperature, or freeze.

- 6 eggs
- 6 tablespoon butter (or dairy free fat), melted
- 4 tablespoon heavy cream or half and half (use coconut milk for dairy free)
- 1 teaspoon vanilla
- 1/2 teaspoon pure stevia powder (equivalent to 1/3 cup pure cane sugar)
- 1/2 teaspoon sea salt
- 1/2 cup coconut flour
- 1/4 cup flaxseed meal
- 1/2 teaspoon baking powder
- 8 ounces fresh raw cranberries
- 4 roasted chestnuts (can substitute with 10 raw pecan or walnut halves)

Cranberry Chestnut Muffins

After you do some holiday baking and roast chestnuts on an open fire, you want to do more! We set aside chestnuts from our annual roasting adventures so I could make these muffins. A recipe for my extra special secret cornbread dressing includes the wonderful inventions of roasted chestnuts and fresh cranberries. I have yet to convince myself to share the recipe, especially since I have not made it in a while, but I did recently have a hankering for the flavors that make up the dressing. The evils of what we call modern day corn have discouraged me from making the dressing in recent years.

To recreate the flavor and texture in a corn free way I came up with these muffins. The flax seed gives them the texture that hints at cornbread (and adds extra fiber), while dancing well with the cranberries and chestnuts. Muffins continue to give Little B a sweet treat while keeping her diet high in fiber and low in sugar. When little she got confused sometimes when she could have muffins at home and not when we were out, but gets it now.

Preheat oven to 400 degrees. Prepare muffin pan with liners or 12 silicon cups on shallow baking pan.

Place eggs, butter, cream, and vanilla in a blender and pulse until combined. Add nuts and cranberries. Blend on low until cranberries and nuts are broken up in small pieces.

In separate bowl combine dry ingredients. Add wet ingredients to dry ingredients and stir just until combined. Divide batter among the 12 muffin cups.

Bake for 15-20 minutes until tops begin to brown. Let cool for about ten minutes before serving.

6 eggs
4 tablespoons plus 2 tablespoons (or 12 1/2 teaspoons) butter (or other fat for dairy free)
2 tablespoons heavy cream (or coconut milk for dairy free)
1/2 teaspoon vanilla
1/4 cup lemon juice
1/2 teaspoon sea salt
1/2 cup coconut flour
1/2 teaspoon pure stevia powder (equivalent to 1/3 cup pure cane sugar)
1/2 teaspoon baking powder
8 ounces blueberries

Blueberry Muffins

Little B used to not like blueberries at all. We stopped even offering them to her, then suddenly, they were the best thing since sliced bread! They still come after blackberries, but they rank pretty high with her these days. This was one of my first recipes using coconut flour. I have since leaned more towards mixing coconut flour with others, like almond flour or flaxseed meal, but the natural sweet and juiciness of the berries keeps the muffins moist. I hope you enjoy the muffins, for we did, in all their blueberry-ness.

Preheat oven to 400F. Prepare muffin pan with liners or 12 silicon muffin cups on shallow baking pan.
In blender pulse together wet ingredients, including blueberries. If you want bulkier pieces of berry, fold the berries along with the dry ingredients instead of the wet.
In separate bowl combine dry ingredients.
Add dry ingredients to wet ingredients and stir just until combined.
Gently fold in blueberries. Divide batter among the 12 muffin cups.
Bake for about 15 minutes until tops begin to brown. Let cool for about ten minutes before serving.

2/3 cup coconut flour
1/2 cup butter
8 large eggs
1/2 teaspoon sea salt
1/2 teaspoon garlic powder
1/2 teaspoon baking powder
1 1/2 cups cheddar cheese, shredded
3 tablespoons fresh jalapeno, chopped

Jalapeño Cheddar Muffins

Holy guacamole these things are good! They also go well with guacamole. Or just butter. Or split and used for a sandwich. Or sliced thinly and toasted and used for tea sandwiches...you probably get that they are very versatile. They are also savory and flavorful. They remind us a lot of the garlic cheddar biscuits an old restaurant chain serves. I don't actually like their seafood, but love their salads and (used to) adore eating the biscuits. When reheating them just brush on some melted garlic butter and you will see what I mean.

In a small dry sauté pan over medium high heat add the jalapeño. Sear and stir for about five minutes, until edges begin to brown. Remove from heat and set aside.

Preheat the oven to 400 degrees. Prepare 12 greased muffin tins or place silicon muffin cups on a shallow baking pan.

Whisk together the coconut flour, salt, and baking powder.

In another bowl, beat the eggs. Whisk in the melted butter.

Add the coconut flour mixture to the egg/butter mixture and stir to combine until it forms a wet dough mixture.

Add seared jalapeños and 1 cup of shredded cheese. Stir until cheese is well distributed.

Divide the batter among muffin cups. Sprinkle the remaining cheese on top of the muffins/loaves.

Bake for 20-25 minutes or until cheese turns golden brown. Let cool slightly before removing from pan.

6 eggs
6 tablespoons butter (or dairy free fat)
2 tablespoons unsweetened coconut milk
1 teaspoon vanilla
5 ounces pureed pumpkin
1/2 teaspoon sea salt
1 teaspoon baking soda
2 teaspoons cinnamon
1/2 teaspoon nutmeg
1/2 teaspoon ground ginger
1/2 cup coconut flour
1/2 teaspoon pure stevia powder
    (equivalent to 1/3 cup pure cane sugar)

Pumpkin Spice Muffins

Oh the sweet smell of autumn! The smell of wood fires. The way the whole world looks like sunset all day long with the changing leaves. The rush to do things in the daylight of shorter days. It is so close I love those days, especially with the windows open and tree tops outside my kitchen window. The smell I most often associate with autumn is spiced pumpkin, whether it is coming from a dish for breakfast, dessert, or a hot beverage. The smell wafting through the air is heavenly. Every evening this week I have set a pot simmering low on the stove with water, vanilla, cinnamon sticks and ginger. The whole house smells like freshly baked pumpkin pie. These are a quick, healthy alternative to the pie version, and no matter how much retailers overdo it on pumpkin spice items, I still like the muffins and pie.

Preheat oven to 400F. Prepare muffin pan with liners or silicon cups on a shallow baking pan.

In a blender combine together eggs, butter, milk, vanilla, pumpkin, and stevia.

In a mixing bowl combine salt, baking soda, cinnamon, nutmeg, ginger, and flour.

Add wet ingredients to dry ingredients and stir just until combined.

Divide batter among the 12 muffin cups. Bake for about 20-25 minutes until tops begin to brown. Let cool for about ten minutes before serving.

1 cup almond flour
1/2 cup coconut flour
1 teaspoon baking soda
1/2 teaspoon sea salt
1/2 teaspoon pure stevia powder
　　(equivalent to 1/3 cup pure cane sugar)
1 teaspoon ground cinnamon
2 ripe bananas
4 tablespoon butter or ghee, melted
6 eggs
1 cup finely ground raw walnuts (optional)

BANANA BREAD

Whenever coconut flour is used it is important to consider the amount of liquid needed to keep it moist. One way to do it is combining it with different flours. In this case, almond flour. The bananas would provide a natural sweetness, and moisture as well, so not much sweetening is needed otherwise. I made a few batches until the flavors were just right. Grinding the walnuts adds to the moisture and sweetness, complementing the banana flavor. As with any banana bread, making it is a great way to use up those darned dark bananas.

Preheat oven to 350 degrees. Line rectangular bread pan with parchment paper, or grease muffin pan (or 12 silicon muffin cups).

In a large bowl combine the almond and coconut flours, baking soda, sea salt, and cinnamon.

In a blender combine the stevia, bananas, eggs, and butter. Purée the banana mixture until smooth. Pour liquid mixture and nuts (optional) to dry mixture. Mix together until combined. Batter will be thick.

Pour batter in bread pan, or divide batter equally in a muffin pan.

Bake in oven for 20-30 minutes. Muffins take about 20 minutes, a loaf about 30. Remove from oven and let cool in pan for about ten minutes. Serve or store in refrigerator.

1 cup cooked, mashed acorn squash
1/2 cup walnuts, finely ground
6 eggs
1/2 cup olive oil
1 tablespoon vanilla extract
1/2 cup coconut flour
1/4 cup golden flaxseed meal
1/2 teaspoon pure stevia powder (equivalent to 1/3 cup sugar)
1 teaspoon sea salt
1 teaspoon baking soda
1/2 teaspoon baking powder
1 teaspoon ground cinnamon
1/4 teaspoon nutmeg

ACORN SQUASH BREAD

I love big beautiful acorn squash. Growing up we had a lot of veggies in our diet, and my favorite squash was the acorn. Most types of squash are great for muffins and breads, so this instance was no different. Of course, I relied on coconut flour and eggs to beef up the protein. Little B likes this stuff a lot, and this particular squash was sweet, so not much was added to make them a hit. Big D bit into it and groaned—in a good way. It reminded him of his grandmother's banana bread, and it had no bananas. Now THAT is a compliment!

Preheat oven to 350 degrees. Grease a bread pan, 8-9 mini loaf pans, or prepare 18 silicon muffin cups.
In blender combine squash, stevia, eggs, oil, and vanilla.
In mixing bowl combine flour, meal, stevia, salt, baking soda, baking powder, cinnamon, and nutmeg. Add blended ingredients to dry ingredients and stir until well mixed.
Pour batter into greased bread pan or 8-9 mini loaf pan(s) or muffin cups. Bake for 40-50 minutes if making one large loaf, or 25-30 minutes for mini loaves or muffins.
The bread is done when the loaves look set (no longer liquid) and the edges begin to brown. Let cool in the pan before removing.

Cornless Cornbread

How do you get cornless cornbread? Don't put corn in it! Big D makes awesome chili and of course cornbread goes great with chili. Alas, the wheat and corn in traditional cornbread aren't the greatest foods in the world to consume. We previously tried to copy cornbread texture with flaxseed meal which did a pretty good job, but I look forward to trying this version next time we make dressing. I cooked these up in a mini muffin pan and easily got 20 muffins out of one batch of batter and cooked them for only 20 minutes—one minute per muffin—go figure. They were a bit on the dry side, compared to actual cornbread I have made in the past, but we easily resolved that issue with a slather of butter on top. Poor us.

- 2/3 cup coconut flour
- 1/2 cup butter
- 8 large eggs
- 1/2 teaspoon sea salt
- 1/2 teaspoon baking powder

Preheat the oven to 400 degrees.
Whisk together the coconut flour, salt, and baking powder.
In another bowl beat the eggs. Whisk in the melted butter.
Add the coconut flour mixture to the egg/butter mixture and stir to combine until it forms a wet dough mixture.
Divide the batter among 12 greased muffin tins or 20 mini muffin tins.
Bake for 20-25 minutes or until golden brown.
Let cool before removing from pan, or burn your fingers by removing them immediately from the pan to split and melt butter on the halves before eating them too soon and burning your tongue.

1 batch cornless cornbread
6 hot dogs

Cornless Corndogs

These are sooooo easy! Whip up a batch of coconut flour 'cornbread,' impale the cornbread muffins with pieces of hot dog, and pop them in the oven. Little B really loves corn dogs, but I don't like giving her the funky ones found in the freezer section of the store or deep fried versions at fast food restaurants.

I'm not saying that when I am surrounded by a carnival, and there is a severe lack of protein or low sugar options, that I am going to deprive her of one. I am just saying that when I have an opportunity to give her (and myself) a more nutritious version, I am going to take it. Though regardless of how nutritious I try to go, they are still hot dogs.

I do try to stick with Hebrew National or uncured versions, but it is still macerated meat. Oh well. Nothing is perfect. Some day I may even figure out how to make these on a stick, but for now, they are delectable muffins. They are baked, portable picnic fare that I personally dip in yellow mustard. Living on the edge. That's me.

Preheat oven to 400 degrees.
Make a batch of cornless cornbread batter.
Divide it equally in a 12-count muffin tin or 18 count mini muffin tin.
Cut each hot dog into two to four pieces. Stick two pieces of hot dog in each muffin (or one in each mini muffin), trying to keep them away from the edges. Bake for approximately 15 minutes, until the batter is cooked and the hot dog pieces are roasted.
Let cool for five minutes before removing from pan. Serve immediately with mustard or refrigerate in an air-tight container.

Desserts

3 ounces coconut butter
2 ounces unsweetened chocolate, chopped
3/4 teaspoon pure stevia powder (equivalent to 1/2 cup pure cane sugar)
2/3 cup cocoa powder
1/4 teaspoon vanilla extract

Sugar Free Chocolate Bar

Dark chocolate is one of my favorite things. It makes me very happy. Chocolate chips have eluded us in our sugar free world—if chips are available at the store they have either sugar or artificial sweeteners we don't eat. Some failures in perfecting this recipe resulted in chocolate that started melting right after removing it from the freezer, or the balance of chocolate and sweet was not quite right.

The coconut butter seems to make a big difference in consistency and flavor. It is made from the meat of the coconut, but with a mild taste. It also stays nice and solid at room temperature, which helps these bars hold up to room temperature adversity. You still get a little meltiness on your fingers when handling it, but what good chocolate bar doesn't melt?

This chocolate bar recipe does not result in perfect little chips with curly peaks, but the resulting small bits that serve the same purpose are lovely. We joyfully toss them into our homemade mint chocolate chip ice cream and cookies. Sweet levels can be adjusted to taste, and the bar also melts smoothly for home mocha lattes or dessert topping. I continue my quest for a curly topped chip, but what is life without a quest?

In a small saucepan add coconut butter and chocolate. Melt over low heat until smooth.

Remove from heat and stir in stevia, cocoa powder, and vanilla. Continue stirring until smooth.

Pour into molds or spread in a pan lined with aluminum foil. An 8x8 size pan makes for the thickness of a typical chocolate bar.

Refrigerate until chocolate sets firm, about one hour.

For chocolate chunks use a sharp knife to chop into small pieces.

2 1/2 cups unsweetened minced coconut
1/2 cup coconut oil
3/4 teaspoons pure stevia powder
    (equal to 1 cup pure cane sugar)
1 cup egg whites
1/2 cup unsweetened coconut milk
1/4 teaspoon sea salt

Coconut Macaroons

Big D is all about things coconut. Well, maybe not ALL things, like blue coconut sno-cones, but definitely about macaroons.
I have discovered recently that my long-standing disregard for coconut was primarily based on exposure to sweetened strips of coconut. You know, the stuff in bags from the baking aisle of the store that are used for cookies and cakes? It is just too pitchy and stringy for my taste. It always made me pucker.

Our discovery of coconut flour as a low carb thickener and baking ingredient has changed my mind. Along with coconut oil I have found that coconut flour and unsweetened coconut meat are great conduits for baking—wheat free, high fiber, low carb tasty treats have come out of our kitchens over the past few years. I eventually got around to making this Big D favorite treat. These macaroons are a little too coconut-y for my taste, but Big D and Little B scarfed them right down—almost the whole batch before lunch! Big D said that after they sat for a day and were chilled they had the chewy middle he loves so much about macaroons, so double yay me.

In a medium sauce pan combine coconut, coconut oil, salt, stevia, and coconut milk. Stir over medium heat until stevia and salt are dissolved. Remove from heat and let cool for about twenty minutes, so the mixture won't cook the egg whites.

Preheat oven to 350F.

Whisk egg whites until they hold shape, but stop before stiff peaks form. Fold egg whites into coconut mixture.

With your hands gently form dough into balls no larger than 1" in diameter or use a small scoop (1 tablespoon portion). Place on baking sheet lined with parchment paper—one batch should make 24-30 macaroons.

Bake for 20-25 minutes, until bottoms begin to brown and tops get brown edges, and to your preferred toastiness. Let cool before removing from parchment.

Store in refrigerator or room temperature in airtight container.

Recipe can be multiplied, and frozen for up to two months.

Cake

    3/4 cup cocoa
    1/2 cup avocado oil
    5 eggs
    2 teaspoons vanilla
    1 teaspoon pure stevia powder (equivalent to 1 1/2 cups pure cane sugar)
    1 cup coconut flour, sifted
    1 tablespoon baking powder (or 2 teaspoons baking soda plus 1/2 teaspoon sea salt)
    1/3 cup heavy cream
    2/3 cup water
    8 ounces cream cheese
    1/2 cup butter or ghee

Frosting

    8 ounces cream cheese, room temperature
    1 teaspoon vanilla
    Dash pure stevia powder
    Food coloring (optional)

Chocolate Cake

This cake recipe was my first foray into using coconut flour when we first began to cut out processed grains and sugar. I made it for Little B's third birthday. The resulting cake is moist and full of the chocolate flavors the birthday girl requested!

Preheat oven to 365 degrees.

In a blender combine eggs, avocado oil, vanilla, heavy cream, water, butter, cream cheese, and stevia.

In separate bowl sift together cocoa, baking powder, and flour. Add the egg mixture to the dry ingredients and whisk together until well combined.

Bake in 9×9 round cake pan for 45-60 minutes. Cake is done when toothpick comes out clean. Let cool in pan for ten minutes before turning it out onto cooling rack.

For cupcakes fill 16-18 silicon muffin cups or lined muffin pans. Cook for 20-25 minutes. Let cool completely before frosting.

To make the frosting whisk together the cream cheese, vanilla and stevia until smooth. For cupcakes frost each one before serving. For the cake spread a thick layer on the top, exposing the sides, or frost the top and sides.

Cake

- 1 cup almond flour
- 2 tablespoons coconut flour
- 1/2 cup cocoa powder
- 2 1/4 teaspoons pure stevia powder (equivalent to 1 1/2 cups pure cane sugar)
- 1 cup unsweetened coconut
- 1 cup pecans, finely chopped
- 4 large eggs
- 1 cup heavy cream
- 1 cup water
- 3 teaspoons vanilla

Topping

- 12 ounces cream cheese, room temperature
- 2 tablespoons coconut oil
- 2 tablespoons heavy cream
- 1 1/2 teaspoon pure stevia powder (equivalent to 1 cup pure cane sugar)
- ½ cup unsweetened coconut
- ½ cup pecans, finely ground

German Chocolate Cake

I came up with this recipe to meet a birthday wish for Big D—nutty, coconutty, chocolatey. Up until this cake, our grain free tendencies prevented him from enjoying one of his favorite cakes: German Chocolate. Although it may seem far from traditional, it met our grain free and sugar free requirements and made for a happy birthday. As always, dairy components can be replaced with your preferred dairy free substitutes.

Preheat oven to 350 degrees.

Place almond flour, coconut flour, cocoa powder, coconut, and pecans into a large bowl. Stir until well combined.

In a separate bowl combine the eggs, stevia, cream, water, and vanilla, stirring thoroughly until the stevia is dissolved. Add the wet ingredients to the dry. Stir until batter is well combined.

Pour into two greased (or lined with parchment paper) 9-inch baking rounds. Bake until solid and firm in the middle. It will not rise very much. Baking time will be 35-45 minutes, depending on your oven. Remove from oven and let cool completely.

Remove rounds from pans and peel off parchment paper.

Make the topping while the cake bakes and cools: combine cream cheese, heavy cream, coconut oil, and stevia in a sauce pan on medium low heat. Heat through and stir until smooth. Set aside and let cool about five minutes. Add coconut and pecans and stir again until well combined. Let topping cool completely.

Place one cake round on a serving plate. Top round with 1/3 of the topping. Place second round on top of first, then finish the cake with remaining topping, spreading it on the sides and top. If you prefer, the topping can go in the middle and on top and not the sides—it should be thick enough to shape smoothly.

Chill to let the topping set. Serve cold or remove from refrigerator about one hour before serving for a softer presentation.

Store leftovers in the refrigerator.

Filling

    2 green apples, peeled and sliced
    2 cups strawberries, stems removed and sliced
    1 teaspoon pure stevia powder (equivalent to 3/4 cup pure cane sugar)
    2 tablespoons lemon juice
    2 teaspoons ground cinnamon

Topping

    1/2 cup almond meal
    1/4 cup golden flaxseed meal
    2 cups finely ground raw pecans
    1/2 cup butter, melted
    3/8 teaspoon pure stevia powder (equivalent to 1/4 cup pure cane sugar)
    1/2 teaspoon sea salt

Apple Strawberry Crisp

This crisp was the closing of a series on German food I did a while back, but I did not necessarily stay close to the traditional German apple crisp, with my use of berries along with apples and cinnamon. According to the numerous people I know who have visited the lovely country it was accurate to think of apple cakes, berry strudels and lederhosen when I concocted it. The 'crumble' top could be thinner, and should be of a thickness you prefer, but I say: why reduce yumminess?!

Preheat oven to 350 degrees.

Place apple and strawberry slices in a medium bowl. Whisk together stevia, lemon juice, and cinnamon until stevia is completely dissolved. Sprinkle mixture over fruit. Toss fruit until it is well coated. Let sit while preparing topping.

Combine the butter, stevia, and salt together until stevia and salt are dissolved. Add the almond meal and ground pecans, then stir until combined.

Divide fruit mixture among four to five single serve ramekins, or place it all in a 9"x9" baking dish. Spread topping over the top, completely covering fruit.

Bake for about 30 minutes, until fruit is bubbly. Cooking time for using a larger baking dish may need to be 45-50 minutes.

Serve plain, with whipped cream or ice cream.

Strawberry Shortcake

Summer is so much about bright, ripe fruit I could strangle myself. I grew up in South Texas, where they have at least a dozen fruit-based festivals every summer—watermelon, blueberry, tomato, peach, grapefruit, cantaloupe, gourd, hot sauce, wine, strawberry...oh wait, some of those aren't fruit, but they might as well be, the way Texans consume them in the summertime. My favorite is strawberries. We would get strawberries by the flat. They would go in our cereal, on our salads, on toast and waffles, and of course dessert. One year I ate so many I got hives while in a movie theater watching Steel Magnolias. First there was the itch, then the welts, then the freaking out because I never had them before and wondering what I caught at work serving frozen yogurt. Friends assured me they would go away and they did, after a day or two. Strawberries were the obvious culprit. It has not happened since, but these days I am very careful when faced with an entire flat of the berries.

Because of the higher carbohydrate count of the stuff, I am also careful, in spite of the fact that they don't fall very short of being the most wonderful stuff on earth. To balance the carbs of berries I have come up with this otherwise pretty low carb dessert. My favorite version is with strawberries, but any berry will do. I took a chance and tweaked some successful almond meal based muffin recipes, in the hope that there would be enough sponginess and firmness to honor the berries. The cake came out wonderfully—moist and cakey but not too dense. You cannot believe how happy I am to have strawberry shortcake in my grain free, lowish carb repertoire!

1 1/2 cups almond meal
1 teaspoon baking soda
1/2 teaspoon salt
3/8 teaspoon pure stevia powder
    (equivalent to 1/4 cup pure cane sugar)
2 eggs
1/2 cup butter, melted and cooled slightly
1 tablespoon lemon juice
1 teaspoon vanilla

Fresh Berries (see below for strawberry version, other berries can be left whole)
Whipped Cream (see step 3 below in strawberry version)

Preheat oven to 350 degrees.

Line the bottom of a 9x9 baking dish with parchment paper, or use 9 silicon jumbo muffin cups.

In a medium bowl combine the almond meal, baking soda, and salt.

In a separate bowl add the eggs, stevia, butter, lemon juice, and vanilla. Stir until completely combined and the stevia is dissolved. Add wet ingredients to the dry and stir until combined.

Pour batter into prepared baking dish and with a spatula even out the top. Bake for 25 minutes, until toothpick comes out clean from the center and the top begins to turn golden. Remove from oven and let cool completely or place in refrigerator until ready to serve. Trying to manipulate it before completely cool or cold will result in a crumbly mess.

Slice in squares or rectangles and layer with whipped cream and berries.

Preparing strawberries for shortcake is a little different from using other berries. Other berries can be left whole and layered with whipped cream and cake. To make a traditional strawberry shortcake take the following steps:

1) Set aside enough pretty, whole berries to put one on top of each planned serving (one cake will serve 6-8).

2) Gather three to four additional berries per person. Slice and dice the berries, tossing them with a splash of lemon juice. Let sit for about ten minutes and the juices will release. Mush them up a bit to add to the sauce.

3) Place one cup heavy whipping cream, 1/2 tsp vanilla extract and a sprinkling of pure stevia powder to a bowl. Whisk them together until cream makes stiff peaks. Double quantities for every four servings. This whipped cream does not have any stabilizers and will not keep for more than a day or so.

4) To prepare the dessert it is recommended that steps are completed in a production line, doing every layer for all servings at the same time, evenly distributing chopped berries and whipped cream. Cut the cake into 6 - 8 pieces. For each serving slice a square of cake in half lengthwise. Place the bottom half on a plate. Drop a spoonful of strawberries on the cake slice and spread, pressing it into the cake a bit. Drop a dollop of whipped cream and another spoonful of berries. Place the top half of the cake square on top and lightly press it down. Add more chopped strawberries, top with a final dollop of cream and finish with a pretty, whole berry.

Serve immediately.

Cake

        4 tablespoons butter
        3 eggs
        4 medium strawberries, cored and chopped
        1 teaspoon vanilla
        1 lemon, juiced with meat
        1 cup almond flour
        1/2 cup golden flaxseed meal
        1/4 teaspoon salt
        1/2 teaspoon baking soda
        3 teaspoons pure stevia powder (equivalent to 2 cups pure cane sugar)
        1/2 cup small quartered strawberries

Strawberry Lemon Cake With Frosting

When Little B was younger, and we were more mobile, we had a tradition of doing a family out of town trip to a beach for her birthday. We had the opportunity to do it on the West Coast, Alaska Coast, East Coast, and Gulf of Mexico. A challenge for each trip was having a sugar free, grain free cake for her on THE day. For her fourth birthday I made in advance of our departure a strawberry lemon cake, which was waiting for her on birthday morning, thanks to a fridge in the hotel room. It traveled well and thankfully I remembered to pack a knife for spreading of the frosting and cutting of the pieces. I must say my plan worked like a dream and the whole thing was inhaled by us all. We kept to our food rules, had fun, and had no sugar/gluten crash. Besides the princess paraphernalia (ugh) and first bicycle (yay), the cake was a favorite that year. The cake has a very different texture compared to the coconut flour cakes elsewhere in this book, but was still delicious. It came out dense, very strawberry, very moist and nice and sweet, just like the birthday girl!

Frosting

- 1 package cream cheese, room temperature
- 1/2 cup butter, room temperature
- 1 1/2 teaspoons pure stevia powder (equivalent to 1 cup pure cane sugar)
- 1/2 cup puréed strawberries

In medium pan over medium heat melt the butter. Continue cooking it until the butter is brown and fragrant. Remove from heat and set aside.

Preheat oven to 350 degrees.

In a blender add eggs, stevia, cored and chopped strawberries, vanilla and lemon juice with meat. Blend until combined and strawberries are puréed.

Place almond flour, flaxseed meal, salt and baking soda in a mixing bowl. Add the contents of the blender and mix until well combined. Add butter and mix again until butter is incorporated.

Line the bottom of a 9-inch round baking dish with parchment paper, or prepare 12 silicon cupcake cups/muffin pan. Pour batter into pan, then drop strawberries into the batter, distributing them evenly.

Bake for 25-30 minutes, or 20-22 minutes for cupcakes. The time may vary based on the juiciness of the strawberries. Remove from oven and let cool in the pan. When cool gently flip cake out of pan and place on serving dish.

Frost as desired. For the strawberry cream cheese frosting noted above, combine all ingredients together and whip until smooth. It may need to be chilled for a few minutes to firm up before spreading on the cake.

Keep cake refrigerated until serving if room temperature is over 75 degrees.

CHOCOLATE CHEESECAKE

This cheesecake has a wonderfully smooth texture. To get it you definitely have to take the time to make sure the cream cheese is well incorporated and no lumps are left.

Crust

>   2 cups finely ground almond flour
>   2 tablespoons coconut flour
>   1 tablespoon butter, melted
>   3/8 teaspoon pure stevia powder (equivalent to 1/4 cup pure cane sugar)
>   1 teaspoon unsweetened cocoa powder
>   1 egg white, lightly whisked

Filling

>   16 ounces cream cheese, room temperature
>   1/3 cup sour cream, room temperature
>   2 eggs, room temperature
>   1 egg yolk (retained from crust ingredients)
>   4 ounces unsweetened chocolate
>   1 1/2 teaspoons pure stevia powder (equivalent to 1 cup pure cane sugar)
>   1/2 teaspoon ground cinnamon
>   1 teaspoon vanilla extract

Preheat oven to 325 degrees.

In 9" pie dish or spring form pan cut a round of parchment paper that fits the bottom of the dish.

Make the crust in a medium bowl by stirring together the almond flour, coconut flour, stevia and cocoa powder. Add the butter and stir until the ingredients clump together. Add the egg white and continue stirring until fully incorporated. Crust will still be crumbly.

Press crust into pie dish until bottom and sides are covered, or the bottom of the spring form pan is covered evenly.

Filling: in large bowl combine stevia, cinnamon, cream cheese, and sour cream until mixture is completely smooth.

Melt chocolate in the microwave proof bowl. Heat and stir in 10 second increments until chocolate is melted and smooth. Add chocolate to cream cheese and sour cream mixture. Whisk together until completely smooth.

Add butter and stir again until smooth.

Add eggs, yolk and vanilla. Stir to incorporate and until smooth.

Pour filling into crust and gently smooth the surface with a spatula.

Place cheesecake in oven on the middle rack. Bake for 30-35 minutes, until filling sets.

Turn off heat without opening oven door. Leave cake in oven until oven and cake are completely cooled, about two hours. Remove from oven and chill for at least an hour.

Leaving it in the oven helps it cool very slowly and and not fall as easily. If you need your oven and unable to leave the cheesecake in the oven the full two hours, then leave it in as long as possible.

Serve plain or with fresh berries.

LIMEY CHEESECAKE

Of all the desserts in all the homes and restaurants and coffee shops I have visited, I am likely to pick cheesecake last. I actually like smooth, flavorful cheesecake, but I have found over time that I am picky and end up finding them icky. I tend not to pick it as my treat of choice because it is easy to make icky cheesecake. For me icky has a specific definition when it comes to cheesecake—that slightly rough, bumpy texture that tastes like something vague, usually plastic or paper, and is far from convincing me to think, 'hmm, I like this.' Enter Big D. He loooooves cheesecake. I actually have not discussed the 'icky' version I tend to experience, but he got a sad little look the other day when we saw some cheesecake in the dessert display of a restaurant. "Can you make some?" he asks hopefully. I say "yes, of course," and his face lights up like a kid with a new bike.

Don't even ask me how many bikes he owns; needless to say, I have seen that look on him plenty of times before. Here is my cheesecake recipe, with no grains or sugar added. I think it turned out great and wish I had tried to make it sooner. No "icky" factor for me this time! I would really disappoint myself if I contributed an icky cheesecake. There is enough of it in the world. And based on Big D's reaction to eating it, I scored big on getting a repeat of the new-bike face.

Crust

- 2 cups finely ground almond flour
- 2 tablespoons coconut flour
- 2 tablespoons butter, melted
- 1/4 level teaspoon pure stevia powder (equivalent to 2 tablespoons pure cane sugar)
- 1 teaspoon ground cinnamon
- 1/4 teaspoon ground nutmeg
- 1/4 teaspoon ground ginger
- 1 egg white, whisked (save yolk for filling)

Filling

- 16 ounces cream cheese, room temperature
- 1/3 cup sour cream
- 2 large eggs and 1 egg yolk, room temperature
- 3 tablespoons butter, room temperature
- 2 tablespoons heavy whipping cream, room temperature
- 1 1/2 teaspoons pure stevia powder (equivalent to 1 cup pure cane sugar)
- 2 large limes, zested and juice separated from meat (use less for milder lime tang)
- 1 teaspoon vanilla extract
- Fresh berries (optional)

Preheat oven to 325 degrees.

In 9" pie dish or spring form pan cut a round of parchment paper that fits the bottom of the dish.

Make the crust in a medium bowl by stirring together the almond flour, coconut flour, stevia, cinnamon, nutmeg and ginger. Add the butter and stir until the ingredients clump together. Add the egg white and continue stirring until fully incorporated. Crust will still be crumbly.

Press crust into pie dish until bottom and sides are covered, or the bottom of the spring form pan is covered evenly.

Filling: in large bowl combine stevia, cream cheese and sour cream until mixture is completely smooth.

Add butter and stir again until smooth.

Add eggs, yolk and vanilla. Stir to incorporate and until smooth.

Add lime zest, lime juice and vanilla. Beat until well combined and smooth.

Pour filling into crust and gently smooth the surface with a spatula.

Place cheesecake in oven on the middle rack. Bake for 30-35 minutes, until filling sets.

Turn off heat without opening oven door. Leave cheesecake in oven until oven and cheesecake are completely cooled, about two hours. Remove from oven and chill for at least an hour.

Leaving it in the oven helps it cool very slowly and and not fall as easily. If you need your oven and unable to leave the cheesecake in the oven the full two hours, then leave it in as long

as possible.
Serve plain or with fresh berries.

KING CHEESECAKE

In past years I have created a myriad of different King Cake-themed treats. This year I almost passed up creating a new treat, but then Big D opened his mouth. I do admit that most times when he does that the result is positive. Other times, not so much. This time when he got a look on his face and was about to talk I held my breath. Really? We don't have enough King Cake possibilities to choose from? Really?! Well, after he finished sharing his idea (aka closed his mouth) I was sold. Really, we don't have enough. More more more! This here treat is a wonderful combination of past creations. I officially say, Big D, here and now, you were right...this time.

The cheesecake is, as always, extremely creamy and satisfying. The crumbly, nutty topping reminds me of the spicy middle of a traditional King Cake, and the colored frosting provides for the traditional colors of Mardi Gras—green, gold and purple.

Laissez les bon temps rouler!!!!!

Crust

    2 cups finely ground almond flour
    2 tablespoons coconut flour
    2 tablespoons butter, melted
    1/4 teaspoon pure stevia powder
        (equivalent to 2 tablespoons pure cane sugar)
    1 teaspoon ground cinnamon
    1/4 teaspoon ground nutmeg
    1/4 teaspoon ground ginger
    1 egg white, whisked (save yolk for filling)

Filling

    16 ounces cream cheese, room temperature
    1/3 cup sour cream
    2 large eggs and 1 egg yolk, room temperature
    3 tablespoons butter, room temperature
    2 tablespoons heavy whipping cream, room temperature

1 1/2 teaspoons pure stevia powder
   (equivalent to 1 cup pure cane sugar)
2 large limes, zested and juice separated from meat (use less for milder lime tang)
1 teaspoon vanilla extract

Topping

1/2 cup raw pecans
1/2 cup raw walnuts
1 tablespoon ground cinnamon
1/4 teaspoon pure stevia powder
   (equivalent to 1/4 cup pure cane sugar)
1/4 cup butter, melted
Dash sea salt

Frosting

4 ounces cream cheese, room temperature
3 ounces butter, room temperature
Dash pure stevia powder
Food coloring (green, yellow, purple—made with one part blue and three parts red)

Topping: Preheat oven to 350 degrees. Spread raw walnuts and pecans in one layer on a shallow, metal baking sheet.

Place in oven for about five to eight minutes, until they begin to darken. Remove from oven, and set aside to cool.

In a microwavable bowl add the butter. Melt on medium power, checking every 30 seconds, until completely melted. Stir in stevia with butter until dissolved.

In food processor grind toasted nuts until they are a consistency of a rough meal. Add to the butter the ground nuts, cinnamon, and salt.

Stir until well combined. Set aside.

Crust: Preheat oven to 325 degrees.

In 9" pie dish or spring form pan cut a round of parchment paper that fits the bottom of the dish.

Make the crust in a medium bowl by stirring together the almond flour, coconut flour, stevia, cinnamon, nutmeg, and ginger. Add the butter and stir until the ingredients clump together. Add the egg white and continue stirring until fully incorporated. Crust will still be crumbly.

Press crust into pie dish until bottom and sides are covered, or the bottom of the spring form pan is covered evenly.

Filling: in large bowl combine cream cheese and sour cream until mixture is completely smooth.

Add stevia to the butter and whisk until dissolved. Add to the cream cheese mixture and stir again until smooth.

Add eggs, yolk and vanilla. Stir to incorporate and until smooth.

Add lime zest, lime juice and vanilla. Beat until well combined and smooth.

Pour filling into crust and gently smooth the surface with a spatula.

Place cheesecake in oven on the middle rack. Bake for 25 minutes, until filling sets.

Remove cake from oven and sprinkle topping on top—either evenly over the the entire top of the cheesecake, or just along the edges, leaving a 2" diameter space in the middle uncovered, like the hole in the middle of a traditional King Cake.

Return cake to oven for 10 more minutes.

Turn off heat without opening oven door. Leave cheesecake in oven until oven and cheesecake are completely cooled, about two hours.

Leaving it in the oven helps it cool very slowly and and not fall as easily. If you need your oven and are unable to leave the cheesecake in the oven the full two hours, then leave it in as long as possible.

Frosting and Decoration: Whisk together cream cheese, butter, and stevia until well combined and smooth. Divide mixture into three separate bowls.

Using green, yellow, and purple food coloring, color the mixture in the different bowls until the desired tint is achieved. Using a spoon for each color drizzle the frosting over the top of the cheesecake—if you left the middle of the cheesecake clear of topping, I suggest you continue the theme of leaving the middle plain and drizzle the frosting over the portions with the topping.

If the frosting is too firm to spread randomly you have two choices: 1) scoop frosting onto the bottom of a spoon and run it over the top of the cake, allowing it to catch on the pieces of topping, or 2) heat the frosting in the microwave at half power for 15-30 seconds until it is runny, then drizzle it over the top of the cake.

If the topping was spread over the top of the entire cheesecake, then use any pattern you choose to apply the frosting.

Chill finished cheesecake at least one hour before serving.

Crust

    1 1/2 cups almond flour
    1 teaspoon ground cinnamon
    3/8 teaspoon pure stevia powder (equivalent to 1/4 cup pure cane sugar)
    4 tablespoons butter, melted

Custard

    15 ounces puréed pumpkin
    1 tablespoon ground cinnamon
    1 teaspoon ground ginger
    1/2 teaspoon ground cloves
    1/4 teaspoon nutmeg
    1/2 teaspoon salt
    1 1/2 teaspoons pure stevia powder (equivalent to 1 cup pure cane sugar)
    2 large eggs
    1 1/4 cups heavy cream

Pumpkin Pie

A pumpkin pie with a crispy crust and moist custard, full of spices and sweetness. A quintessential dessert around my house during the holidays. We like serving it chilled, and mine is usually topped with some freshly whipped cream. I like making it first thing in the morning so the house smells wonderful all day. Little B is becoming quite a pro at stirring, so the custard was a joint effort this year. Sometimes I use fresh pumpkin, other times I resort to canned stuff. I have discovered over the years that the fresh stuff needs a little more spicing to get that just-right balance of flavors in the pie. Big D likes his pumpkin pie extra spicy and wheat free, while I want it sugar free with a flaky crust. This recipe met all four requirements! My next wheat free, sugar free pie will be pecan. Stay tuned!

Preheat oven to 375°F.

For the crust, mix together the almond flour, stevia and butter until combined. Press mixture into a 9-inch pie plate and refrigerate for at least 30 minutes.

In a medium bowl whisk pumpkin purée, stevia, cinnamon, ginger, cloves, and salt to combine.

Mix in eggs, one at a time. Add heavy cream and mix well.

Pour custard into pie crust. Cover crust edge with aluminum foil or pie crust shield.

Bake for about 40 minutes, or until filling is set but not cracking in the middle. Cool on a wire rack.

Serve room temperature or chill prior to serving, as desired.

Cakes

    6 eggs
    ½ cup butter, room temperature
    1 teaspoon vanilla
    ¼ cup coconut flour
    ½ cup golden flaxseed meal
    ¼ cup cocoa powder
    1 teaspoon pure stevia powder
        (equivalent to 3/4 cup pure cane sugar)
    1 teaspoon baking soda
    ½ teaspoon sea salt
    1 teaspoon ground cinnamon

Frosting

    1 8 ounce block cream cheese, room temperature
    ½ cup butter, room temperature
    ½ teaspoon vanilla
    ¼ cup cocoa powder
    3/4 teaspoon pure stevia powder
        (equivalent to 1/2 cup pure cane sugar)

Double Chocolate Cupcakes

These cupcakes came from the mouth of my babe, Little B. One day she got a baking hankering and we followed it through. Little chocolate cupcakes with chocolate frosting that don't have any wheat or sugar. She is adamant about those two points, which meant we got to create a new recipe..."with only really good tasting ingredients, Mommy. Don't forget they have to be really good," she tells me. Well, they are really good, and buttery and rich. Also a chance to crack eggs and spread frosting, which are always good things. Really good things.

Preheat oven to 350 degrees.
Combine eggs, stevia, butter, and vanilla in a medium bowl. Whisk together until combined.
In a separate bowl combine flour, meal, cocoa powder, salt, baking soda, and cinnamon. Add dry ingredients to egg mixture and stir until well combined.
Divide batter among a lined 12 regular sized or 24 mini muffin pan.
Bake for 17-20 minutes until tops are firm. Remove from oven and let cool completely.
For the frosting add the cream cheese, stevia, vanilla, and butter in a medium bowl. Whisk until combined. Add cocoa and continue whisking until combined. Chill a few minutes if it comes out thin.
Spread frosting over cupcakes. Store cupcakes in the refrigerator until serving—mostly to keep the frosting firm, otherwise they can sit at room temperature.

Cakes

    1 pound strawberries, cored
    1 tablespoon lime juice
    1 teaspoon pure stevia powder
        (equivalent to 3/4 cup pure cane sugar)
    6 eggs
    1 tablespoon vanilla
    3/4 cup coconut flour
    1/4 cup golden flaxseed meal
    1 1/2 teaspoons baking soda
    1/2 teaspoon sea salt

Strawberry Cream Cheese Frosting

    8 ounces cream cheese, room temperature
    ½ cup salted butter, room temperature
    3/4 teaspoon pure stevia powder
        (equivalent to 1/2 cup pure cane sugar)
    2 tablespoons puréed cored strawberries

Strawberry Cupcakes

These cupcakes taste like summer, even if you have to use frozen strawberries in the middle of winter. They are full of flavor, and with the fiber and protein content of coconut flour and flaxseed meal they are surprisingly filling treats.

Preheat oven to 350 degrees.
In a blender or food processor add the strawberries and lime juice. Blend until strawberries are smooth and no large pieces remain. Set aside 2 tablespoons.
Add stevia and eggs to the strawberry mixture and blend longer until well combined.
In a separate bowl combine the coconut flour, flaxseed meal, baking powder, and salt. Add the wet ingredients to the dry and mix some more until combined. Let the batter sit for a few minutes—you will notice the coconut flour thickens it a bit.
Pour batter into 24 mini muffin tins or 12 regular muffin cups. Bake for 20-25 minutes until set and browning.
While the cupcakes are baking prepare the frosting. In a small bowl combine the puréed strawberries and stevia until the stevia is dissolved. In a medium bowl combine the the cream cheese and butter. Stir the strawberry mixture with the cream cheese mixture until combined.
When cupcakes are cooled frost them. Store covered in the refrigerator.

For the Cakelettes

      6 eggs
      4 tablespoons heavy cream
      1 teaspoon vanilla
      1/2 teaspoon sea salt
      2/3 cup coconut flour
      1/4 cup golden flaxseed meal
      3/4 teaspoon pure stevia powder (equivalent to 1/2 cup
           pure cane sugar)
      1 teaspoon baking soda
      1 cup pecans, shelled

KING CAKELETTES

When Mardi Gras is near we always want to celebrate it, wherever we are. After living in New Orleans a few years back we cannot help but get in the spirit of Mardi Gras. There is never a lull down there after Christmas—the frivolity of New Years quickly turns to the Mardi Gras celebrations. Parades begin in mid-January so there is no time to waste.

Some years I have done a cake marathon, making sure everyone in the house had some for celebrating. I made a regular, yeasty, cinnamon-y king cake, including sharing of details about king cake history, followed by a gluten free version of the cake. They were both delectable and fun to make.

More recently Mardi Gras still arrived as it does every year, but during a time when we are avoiding sugar, wheat and carbohydrates. What is a girl to do? Well, adapt. That is what she does. I used my experimenting with low carb muffins over the years and incorporated my love of king cakes into these little treats.

Although not the traditional ring with colored sugar, the result definitely has the right flavors and textures in play. I usually avoid making king cakes most of the year, but this time I may not. These things are stupendous and did not even last us through Fat Tuesday. Enjoy!

For the Filling

6 tablespoons butter or ghee, melted
3/8 teaspoon pure stevia powder (equivalent to 1/4 cup pure cane sugar)
1 teaspoon cinnamon
1/2 cup pecans

For the Icing

3 tablespoons water
3 teaspoons lime or lemon juice

3/4 teaspoon pure stevia powder
     (equivalent to 1/2 cup pure cane sugar)
Green, yellow, red and blue (2 drops blue, 3 drops red for purple) food coloring (optional, if coloring icing instead of using colored sugar)

For Decorating

Divide the icing into three separate small bowls and add food coloring to each.

Preheat oven to 400 degrees.
On a baking pan spread out pecans in one layer. Bake in oven for about 5 minutes until they begin to brown.
Prepare silicon muffin cups or a muffin pan with liners.
In blender add the eggs, heavy cream, vanilla, stevia, and nuts together. Blend on low until nuts are broken up into small pieces.
In separate mixing bowl combine coconut flour, golden flaxseed meal, salt, and baking soda.
Add wet ingredients to dry ingredients and stir just until combined.
Divide batter among the muffin cups.
For the filling mix together in a small bowl butter, stevia, and cinnamon. In a food processor grind into a powder the 1/2 cup pecans and combine with other filling ingredients.
With a teaspoon drop some filling into the middle of each muffin. It will sink a bit and be covered by the muffin batter during the baking time. Bake for about 15-18 minutes until tops begin to brown.
While the muffins are baking make the icing. Combine the water, lime juice, and stevia until smooth. If coloring the icing, divide the icing into three different batches and add colors accordingly.
A soon as the muffins come out of the oven drizzle the icing on top.
Serve at room temperature. Refrigerate or freeze and gently heat in the microwave before serving.

1 cup pumpkin purée
1/2 cup heavy whipping cream
3 large eggs
1 tablespoon ground cinnamon
1 teaspoon ground ginger
1/2 teaspoon sea salt
1/4 teaspoon ground clove
3/4 teaspoon pure stevia powder (equivalent to 1/2 cup pure cane sugar)
Whipped heavy whipping cream to serve (optional)

Pumpkin Custard

I rarely make my own puréed pumpkin. I used to, but it was much more labor intensive than I wanted to deal with. By the time I baked it and smoothed out all the stringiness I was tired of dealing with the stuff. I am hooked on using already smooth and prepared pumpkin (which often is not purely pumpkin, but includes other types of squash that are less stringy). I use very few prepared ingredients when I cook, but some I do rely on consistently. Besides pumpkin, I rely on prepared tomatoes and tomato sauces, as well as artichoke hearts. I will leave the time and effort needed to prepare them to other people. That way I can focus on making other stuff and doing funner things.

Unlike other desserts, a custard like this is high in protein and goes great as breakfast too!

Preheat oven to 325 degrees.

In a medium bowl whisk together the eggs, stevia, and whipping cream. Add pumpkin purée, cinnamon, ginger, salt, and clove, whisking well to incorporate all the ingredients. Divide the custard evenly between three 1-cup ramekins.

Place ramekins, evenly spaced, in a 9×13 baking dish. Fill dish with water so ramekins are submerged half way up.

Place dish in preheated oven on the middle rack. Bake for 30-35 minutes, until centers of all ramekins are firm.

Serve immediately, topped with whipped cream, or chill and serve cold.

This recipe can easily be doubled or tripled to make more individual servings.

BEVERAGES

EGGNOG

Some may be freaked out about this recipe. Not because it is eggy and not because it is boozy, but because it is RAW. You might get a bit antsy about consuming raw eggs, but we live on the edge. I do like the taste of cooked eggnog, but in my opinion it's often dominated by the alcohol taste. Overall I much prefer the raw version—I can taste all the different flavors mixing together in each sip. It is frothy right out of a blender, and nice and smooth after it sits in the fridge for an hour or two. Do not fear, for it can still be boozy if you want it to be; it can also not be as obvious.

We usually make it between November and January. I have thought about making it other times of the year, but it seems wrong. Big D has perfected the ratios over the years.

Well, here it is. I hope you enjoy it!

    10 eggs
    2 cups heavy whipping cream
    1 1/2 teaspoons pure stevia powder (equivalent to 1 cup pure cane sugar)
    1 teaspoon ground nutmeg
    1 tablespoon vanilla extract
    1/2 cup spiced rum*
    1/4 cup whiskey*
    Additional ground nutmeg for garnish.

Combine all ingredients in a blender. Blend on high for 10 seconds. Let eggnog sit for five minutes. Serve immediately, sprinkled with nutmeg, or refrigerate until time to serve.

*Alcohol can be replaced by rum extract to taste, or excluded entirely

Hot Cocoa Mix

Sitting on the balcony on a foggy, cold winter night there is nothing finer than a cup of hot cocoa and plate of warm cookies while curled up under a thick blanket. In the process of watching my carb and sugar intake I missed the most the lovely smooth taste of that hot cocoa during the winter. Not any more.

I finally found a sturdy combination of flavors that satisfies my hot cocoa craving: not too sharp or too sweet, while avoiding a total diet ruination.

The mix is versatile enough to go with whole milk for Little B, with coconut milk for Big D, or with combined water and heavy cream for my favorite version. It is rich and smooth and I don't even miss the marshmallows.

It can even be sprinkled into coffee to make a lovely mocha. Yum!

 1 cup unsweetened cocoa powder
 2 teaspoons pure stevia powder
    (equivalent to 1 1/2 cups pure cane sugar)
 1 teaspoon sea salt
 1/2 teaspoon ground nutmeg

In a food processor add cocoa powder, stevia, salt, and nutmeg. Blend on high until stevia and cocoa are well combined. Store in airtight container at room temperature.

For a cup of hot cocoa you will need 1 cup of liquid. I have experimented with the different liquid combinations listed below:

 1 cup milk, or
 1 cup unsweetened coconut milk, or
 1/2 cup water, 1/2 cup heavy cream, or
 1/2 cup water, 1/4 cup heavy cream, 1/4 cup coconut milk

To make cocoa stir in 1 tablespoon of cocoa mix with 1/2 cup of liquid until dissolved. Heat for 20 seconds. Add the additional 1/2 cup of liquid and stir. Heat for 60-90 more seconds until hot.

Stir one more time. Enjoy!

AFTERWORD

I am excited to have finished my first cookbook. It is a piece of a story that continues. My friends and family still eat food every day, including nutrient dense ingredients as shown here, and in combinations that help us as much or more than any medication could.

At least so far! Maybe someday there will be a magic pill that means we won't have to be careful about what we eat. But even if that's true, will it really be an improvement? At least for us, food is important in our lives and we will never want to stop learning about it, respecting it, and passing on what we find as we go along.

In the future I plan to do more cookbooks, and of course more cooking as well! If you would like to keep up with what happens next, you can sign up for my mailing list or keep tabs directly through my company website, grainfreehaven.com.

Thanks for dipping your toes into our grain free and sugar free world, and I hope the more personal bits help to show a little bit about how we integrate these foods into our lifestyle. (Hmm... maybe that will become another book!)

I am expecting most buyers of this book will meet me in person, at a Farmers' Market or elsewhere. But for those people who don't live nearby, an honest online review might help them evaluate this cookbook for their own needs. If you have the time, I would appreciate it very much if you would post your thoughts.

Mostly I hope my efforts will help make your journey easier. I know it works for us!

www.ingramcontent.com/pod-product-compliance
Lightning Source LLC
Chambersburg PA
CBHW040210020526
44112CB00040B/2865